Praise for *Joyful Singing*

"The song of the church comes to us in many and various ways. Benjamin Kolodziej deserves deep thanks for his account of a faithful way among Texas Lutherans. Lutherans and others will benefit from this history and its insights."
—Paul Westermeyer, emeritus professor of church music at Luther Seminary and MSM director with St. Olaf College

"*Joyful Singing* is an engaging, extensively documented history of church music in Lutheranism in Texas, especially as it has unfolded in churches associated with the Lutheran Church-Missouri Synod and its Concordia College in Austin."
—Donald Rotermund, minister of music emeritus, Zion Lutheran Church, Dallas, Texas

"Kolodziej's *Joyful Singing* takes the reader deep into the heart of Texas' music-making among Lutherans, especially its beginnings in the midnineteenth century. His examination of primary sources provides a rare glimpse into the challenges that the Wendish and German immigrants faced and how those early struggles would blossom into a rich and varied practice today."
—Paul Grime, dean of the chapel, Concordia Theological Seminary, Fort Wayne, Indiana

"Benjamin Kolodziej has skillfully woven the pieces of an engaging narrative of LCMS origins and life in Texas. He achieves the rare feat of providing a monograph that is both meticulously documented and an enjoyable read. Kolodziej's research reminds us that the unique Texas landscape provided not only ample space for the larger Baptist, Methodist, and Catholic faith communities but a refuge for the smaller, sturdy, and resilient Lutherans seeking religious freedom. The author puts a face on the Lutheran presence through copious photographs of key figures, churches, organs, and musical collections. This monograph is a study not just for Lutheran pastors and church musicians but for anyone who enjoys a beautifully written history of how faith sprang up in the Texas soil."

—C. Michael Hawn, University Distinguished
Professor Emeritus of Church Music,
Southern Methodist University

"With writing that is winsome and witty, Kolodziej's engaging work offers a wonderful glimpse into the life and work of Lutheran church musicians in Texas. He offers us a true gift—focused, substantive historical insight and profound, applicable theological discernment."

–Rev. Dr. James F. Marriott, Kreft Chair of Music Arts,
Concordia Seminary, St. Louis

"Benjamin Kolodziej can wring water from a stone. Early sources of Lutheran music in Texas are few, but Kolodziej nonetheless spins a convincing narrative from a paucity of information, filling in details through some clever deductions. This exemplary study of local music history should serve as a model for others in a similar vein."

—Joseph Herl, professor of music, Concordia University,
Nebraska, and research professor, University of Illinois at
Urbana-Champaign

Joyful Singing

Shaping American Lutheran Church Music

This is the tenth in a series of monographs—Shaping American Lutheran Church Music—published by the Center for Church Music, Concordia University Chicago, River Forest, Illinois, highlighting people, movements, and events that have helped shape the course of church music among Lutherans in North America.

Joyful Singing

A Story of Lutheran Sacred Music in Texas

Benjamin A. Kolodziej

Fortress Press
Minneapolis, Minnesota

JOYFUL SINGING
A Story of Lutheran Sacred Music in Texas

Published under the auspices of:
Center for Church Music
Concordia University Chicago
River Forest, IL 60305-1402

Cover image: A. G. Ritter, ed., Choral-Buch zu den in der Provinz Brandenburg gebräuchlichen Gesangbüchern, Op. 36 (Erfurt, Germany: Gottfhilf Wilhelm Körners Verlag, 1859): hymn 95, available at Deutsche Digitale Bibliothek, https://www.deutsche-digitale-bibliothek.de/item/ 4Q26MAUSNBCX7AUSFPPVBALYX2C52XXG
Cover design: Savanah Landerholm

Print ISBN: 978-1-5064-8616-1
eBook ISBN: 978-1-5064-8617-8

Contents

About the Center for Church Music

The Center for Church Music was established in 2010 on the campus of Concordia University Chicago. Its purpose is to provide ongoing research and educational resources in Lutheran church music, especially in the areas of congregation song and composition for the church. It is intended to be of interest to pastors, musicians, and laity alike.

The center maintains a continually expanding resource room that houses the Schalk American Lutheran Hymnal Collection, the manuscript collections of prominent Lutheran composers and hymn writers, and a broad array of reference works and resources in church music. To create global awareness and facilitate online research, efforts are underway to digitize the hymnal collection, the manuscripts archives, and the hymn festival recordings.

The center publishes monographs and books covering various aspects of Lutheran church music. The center maintains a dynamic website whose features include devotions, presentations, oral histories, biographical essays, resource recommendations, and conversations on various topics in worship and church music.

The center's founders group includes Linda and Robert Kempke, Nancy and Bill Raabe, Mary and Charles Sukup, and

Waldemar B. Seefeldt, whose significant monetary gifts initiated the center and have, along with the gifts of many others, sustained its momentum.

The center's advisory board includes James Freese, Scott Hyslop, Linda Kempke, Jonathan Kohrs, Nancy Raabe, Tim Schalk, Steven Wente, and Paul Westermeyer.

Barry L. Bobb serves as the center's volunteer director.

You can follow news about the center on Facebook. Learn more about the center and subscribe to its free e-newsletter at http://cuchicago.edu/about-concordia/center-for-church-music.

Acknowledgments

My father's family first arrived in Texas in 1854. These were faithful Polish Catholics who emigrated from Opole, in Silesia, to settle in Panna Maria, southeast of San Antonio, where they would till the earth. They contended with heat, humidity, and rattlesnakes as they eked out a living, raising their families and keeping their old Polish customs with the utmost fidelity, and doing so well into the twentieth century, my grandparents being among the last to speak a nineteenth-century Silesian Polish dialect. The year 1854 also brought many other immigrants to Texas, including the Lutheran Wends who would establish the Lutheran Church–Missouri Synod (LCMS) in the state, bringing with them their confessional Lutheranism and ethnic customs, which, like the Polish, they would jealously preserve in their new homeland. The historic Wendish capital city of Bautzen in Upper Lusatia lies just 180 miles from the Polish Silesian city of Opole, and unbeknown to them, my ancestors would settle in Texas only about 120 miles from the Wendish community, who themselves settled farther east in more fertile lands. Although both the Texas Polish and the Texas Wends would have bristled at the suggestion that they bore much in common, they truly did. Both cultures cherished the free exercise of their religion, which was increasingly difficult to practice in Europe and directly motivated their emigration. Both cultures sought the opportunities and independence that Texas seemed to afford, and the leaders of neither group truly understood the difficulties they would encounter.

My mother's family comes from secure Lutheran stock, my great-grandfather having come to Texas in 1904 as a Lutheran missionary, a pastor trained at the seminary of St. Chrischona outside of Basel, Switzerland. In Texas, he joined the Texas Synod rather than the Missouri Synod, but the ministry of Rev. Gottlieb Walter unfolded throughout the heart of Central Texas, where so many Lutherans were already living. My mother, Annamarie Kolodziej, has spent much of her life researching these Lutheran churches and early pastors in Central Texas, and I remember many a family vacation being spent, at least in part, exploring country church cemeteries and driving down rural Texas country roads from town to town, each with seemingly exotic names that bore an imprint of Old Europe: New Bern, Wutrich Hill, and Noack, to name just a few. Her cataloging of the histories of these country churches—which usually involved collecting those self-printed church histories that are as ubiquitous as the plush, red, sound-absorptive carpet in their associated sanctuaries—has proven a significant resource as I began research into Texas Lutheran music. Her research laid the groundwork for mine in this book, and it is proper that I thank her first.

Likewise, I am grateful to librarian and docent Marian Wiederhold and for the other staff at the Texas Wendish Heritage Museum in Serbin, Texas, who provided access to some important primary source documents. Jack Wiederhold, organist emeritus at St. Paul Lutheran in Serbin, provided ongoing assistance in interpreting these sources, all while helping me understand the unique liturgical praxis of that congregation. There is no one who knows more about early pipe organs in Wendish Texas than he. Jeremy Clifton, purveyor of the social media site Texas Lone Star Back Roads, professional photographer, and editor of the Texas Wendish Heritage Society newsletter, scoured the Serbin archives for pictures related to my topic and has assured us that the likenesses of some of these early Lutheran organists and Texas pioneers will live on. I would like to thank Marcus Dahm, German church musician and scholar, without whose help unraveling the mysteries of nineteenth-century German script I would likely not have been able to decipher many of the annotations in Jan Kilian's *Choralbuch*. Dr. Donald Rotermund, Minister of Music Emeritus at Zion Lutheran in Dallas, and a friend, teacher, and mentor since my own high school days, generously gave of his time—and memories—to this project. Having been active in Texas LCMS music since 1955, his wisdom has emerged from his lived experience, which he has always freely shared. Catherine Burkhard, former archivist at Zion, Dallas, graciously shared records relating to early North Texas Lutherans, while Robert and Kathy Achterberg of Austin provided much source material on the history of St. Paul in Austin. George Nielsen, Emeritus Distinguished Professor of History at Concordia Chicago and biographer and scholar of Jan Kilian and the Texas Wends, offered invaluable advice as I tried to understand the complicated life and complex motivations of Kilian in particular. Harold Rutz, Emeritus Professor of Music at Concordia University, Austin, and a personal mentor of mine for three decades, served as an invaluable resource for this study. Ever humble, Professor Rutz exemplified the ideal Lutheran *servant musician*, always more interested in encouraging others than in building himself up. His contributions to this study were all offered during what turned out to be the final year of his most productive life. God's hand was certainly at work here, allowing me to document the accomplishments in the Lord's vineyard of one of his most committed servants. It is unfortunate that I cannot list here all who assisted with this project, as untold numbers of pastors, musicians, and laypeople, both Lutheran and otherwise, contributed in significant ways to the preparation of this volume.

This entire project owes its very existence to Barry Bobb, director of the Center of Church Music at Concordia Chicago, who encouraged my efforts in documenting Texas Lutheran music, seeing it as a worthy project associated with my appointment as a Schalk Scholar at the center. I note with gratitude Carl Schalk's own contribution to this volume. Although the exigencies of a worldwide pandemic limited our interactions during the preparation of this book to long phone calls, he seemed as genuinely interested in this topic as I was and gave particular insights into the professional development of the church music vocation in the United States throughout the last seventy years. Not only had he lived through these times; his role as a teacher, mentor, and scholar meant that he himself had shaped the Lutheran sacred music profession in a significant way. He had looked forward to reading this book, and I greatly lament that our future collaborations he had brainstormed will no longer be. Nonetheless, I think it proper to dedicate this book to Carl Schalk, whose contributions to American Lutheranism will stand for generations. "Well done, thou good and faithful servant."

Finally, I wish to thank my parents, Eddie and Annamarie Kolodziej, for instilling in me a love for the church and its history, and my wife, Carrie, who always supports and encourages my research eccentricities and who sacrificed greatly so that we could traipse around Texas learning the stories of the old Lutherans.

What better way to begin this book than with the hymn that those first Lutheran missionaries from Switzerland sang after they landed in Texas in November 1851 as they were about to go their separate ways to spread the gospel:

Jesus, geh voran
auf der Lebensbahn;
und wir wollen nicht verweilen,
Dir getreulich nachzueilen,
führ uns an der Hand
bis ins Vaterland.

Benjamin A. Kolodziej
Ambleside
Richardson, Texas
Pentecost, 2021

Joyful Singing

1

Lutheran Musical Antecedents in Texas

In 1851, from his office at the Pilgermission St. Chrischona, situated on the bucolic, rolling hills outside of Basel, Switzerland, seminary administrator Christian Spittler wrote an entreaty to supporters for the financial provision of a relatively new missionary venture. Under Spittler's auspices, the St. Chrischona evangelical training school had sent missionaries throughout the world, which most recently had included an ambitious enterprise in Jerusalem—which he had had to abandon. Now, though, his concern turned to a place even farther removed than the Middle East and for which success was even less assured. He informed his benefactors that "six brothers are leaving for Texas, and much equipment is required. Some kind help for this task would strengthen my weak faith. . . . Their help will be necessary for these six men to set up a little church with God's help and later proselytize among the Indians."[1] The previous year, Spittler had sent two missionaries, Adam Sager and Theobald Kleis, charged with surveying the needs of this vast mission field, complete with its recalcitrant colonists, blistering summer heat, stifling humidity, and an

---

1 Johannes Kober, *Christian Friedrich Spittler's Leben* (Basel, Switzerland: Verlag von C. S. Spittler, 1887): 244.

Figure 1.1 Pilgermission St. Chrischona, an evangelical training facility on the outskirts of Basel, Switzerland. (Source: C. F. Schlienz, *The Pilgrim Missionary Institution of St. Chrischona* [London: John Farquhar Shaw, 1850]: frontispiece.)

impertinent native population that was anything but receptive to the Christian faith.

Lutherans had been in Texas less than a decade when Sager and Kleis arrived to evaluate the situation in 1850. Henri de Castro, a French diplomat of Jewish-Portuguese extraction, had become an American citizen and, while consul general for Texas president Sam Houston, had launched a campaign to recruit immigrants to Texas. The country—for Texas was an independent nation from 1836 to 1846—offered generous land grants for European colonists to settle and farm the land.[2] Eventually administered by the Mainzer Adelsverein, some 2,100 immigrants from German territories, Swiss cantons, and the Alsace arrived in Galveston between 1842 and 1847, eventually settling in the rolling hills of Central Texas, west of San

2 Johannes Mgebroff, *Ersten Deutschen Evangelisch-Lutherischen Synode in Texas* (Austin, TX: Selbst-Verlag der Synode, 1902): 4.

Figure 1.2 The Vereinskirche in Fredericksburg, Texas, represents a transplanted northern European architectural style. (Source: Walter F. Edwards, *The Story of Fredericksburg* [Fredericksburg, TX: Fredericksburg Chamber of Commerce, 1969]: 14.)

Antonio, where they established the colonies of Fredericksburg and New Braunfels, among others. The Alamo had fallen a mere six years before the first colonists' arrival, and conditions were primitive, but the industrious Teutons worked the land, building the necessary infrastructure. The first public building in Fredericksburg, the Vereinskirche—built in 1847 as a combination church, schoolhouse, and town hall—is notable for its Carolingian architecture, its eight-sided design reminding the colonists not only of their cultural heritage (it is reminiscent of the court chapel at Aachen) but also of their spiritual legacy, the eight-sided iconography a traditional symbol of baptism.[3] This perhaps represented an attempt to bring their own culture to the forests and plains of Texas, establishing a Germanic civilization in which the church had represented the cornerstone of daily life.[4]

Naturally, to re-create the civic and ecclesiastical culture of Europe in the expanses of Texas, one needed spiritual leadership, a prerequisite that Spittler at St. Chrischona had endeavored to fulfill. It was in this environment that Sager and Kleis had ministered and into which Spittler would soon send six more shepherds for the flocks. Ultimately, the seminary would send over 120 missionaries to Texas between 1850 and the first decade of the twentieth century.[5]

The Earliest Lutheran Music in Texas

The reconstruction of the liturgical life of these early pioneers in Texas is fraught with difficulty for lack of records. These immigrants hailed from various German states, representing the Reformed, Lutheran, and Roman Catholic traditions, their own cultural background nuanced in differences rather than

---

3 Martin Donell Kohout, "Vereins-Kirche," Handbook of Texas Online, https://www.tshaonline.org/handbook/entries/vereins-kirche (accessed September 14, 2020).

4 Although it is true that the Lutheran, Catholic, and Reformed faiths were an integral part of many of the colonists' lives and informed their cultural priorities, there were still quite a few "freethinkers," inheritors of the rationalist philosophies in vogue at the time, who rejected ecclesiastical influence and who labored for a society free from ecclesiastical strictures.

5 Unpublished research compiled by the author's mother as part of family research in the 1990s. This writer's great-grandfather, Gottlieb Walter, was trained at St. Chrischona from 1897 to 1901 before arriving in Texas, where he served a number of churches in the Evangelical Lutheran Texas Synod. He served as the treasurer of the Texas Synod from 1915 to 1922.

monolithic in vision. At the instigation of the two St. Chrischona missionaries and through the leadership of Rev. Caspar Braun, an 1847 St. Chrischona graduate who had been sent to Texas after a term in Pennsylvania,[6] the First Evangelical Lutheran Synod of Texas (hereafter, Texas Synod) was founded in Houston in 1851, aligning itself with the old General Synod, which itself issued from the patriarch Heinrich Melchior Muhlenberg during the days after the American Revolution.[7]

Liturgical uniformity was a priority to these Lutherans, and early on, the Texas Synod adopted the General Synod's liturgy and the 1849 *Deutsches Gesangbuch für die Evangelisch-Lutherische Kirche in den Vereinigten Staaten*, known informally as the Wollenweber Gesangbuch, after its Philadelphia-based

---

6 "Rev. Casper Messon Braun," Findagrave.com, https://www.findagrave.com/memorial/15122938/casper-messon-braun (accessed September 14, 2020). From the Texas historical marker at his grave:

> Braun, a native of Germany was born on March 16, 1822. He studied for the Lutheran ministry at St Chrischona Pilgrim Mission in Basel, Switzerland and became the 11th graduate on March 11, 1847. He came to the United States as a missionary in 1846 and in 1847 was the first pastor of the Beaver Mission in Beaver County. He organized the First German Evangelical Lutheran Church (later known as St. Paul's) in Lawrence County, Penn. on Aug 27, 1849 with 27 members in the congregation. He resigned from St. Paul's in December 1849 and the following year decided to concentrate his efforts in Texas, making the long trip by boat from Pennsylvania to Galveston. He then made his way, like many immigrants, up the bay to the landing at the foot of Main St in Houston. The following year he organized the first German Evangelical Lutheran Church in Houston and was elected president of the German Evangelical Synod of Texas. He was not only a preacher and pastor, but served as a physician and teacher as well. He died suddenly on Oct 14, 1880 at the age of 57.

7 A. G. Wiederaenders, W. A. Flachmeier, and Russell A. Vardell, "Lutheran Church," Handbook of Texas Online, https://www.tshaonline.org/handbook/entries/lutheran-church (accessed September 14, 2020).

Figure 1.3 Rev. Caspar Braun served as the first president of the Texas Synod. (Source: "Notable Interred," Glenwood Cemetery, Houston, TX, https://glenwoodcemetery.org/wp-content/uploads/2020/02/Braun-Casper.jpg [accessed February 2, 2022].)

publisher.[8] The "Württembergische Gesangbuch" had provided much of the source material for the Wollenweber Gesangbuch, as it had for Muhlenberg's *Erbauliche Liedersammlung* over half a century prior. The *Choralbuch für die evangelische Kirche in Württemberg*, first published in 1844, served as the musical companion for organists and choirs whose congregations

---

8 Mgebroff, *Ersten Deutschen*: 130, 211.

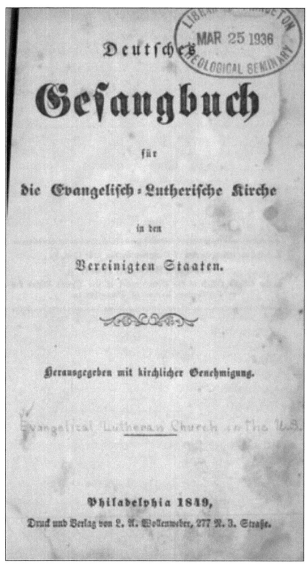

Figure 1.4 The Wollenweber Gesangbuch continued in the
tradition of "mainstream" American Lutheranism as established
by Heinrich Melchior Muhlenberg. (Source: *Deutsches Gesangbuch
für die Evangelisch-Lutherische Kirche in den Vereinigten Staaten*
[Philadelphia: Wollenweber, 1849].)

utilized the Wollenweber Gesangbuch. This *Choralbuch*, containing 210 tunes to supply the 710 texts in the hymnal, mostly employs the isorhythmic versions of the tunes, favoring the ponderously reverent to the invigoratingly joyful.[9] Musical leadership was probably minimal given the strictures of pioneer society, but likely reed organs, so ubiquitous on the American frontier for their light weight and durability, supplied much of the musical leadership. However, these early missionaries were so committed to the importance of music in the spiritual life of these early Texan Lutherans that they brought over at least one pipe organ to aid in the task.

In 1958, Texas organ builder Rubin Frels happened upon an old railroad depot in the small hamlet of Raisin, Texas, located between Houston and San Antonio, inland from the coast. Within this inhospitable structure had lain, apparently for some time, a small, decrepit chamber organ of curious construction. It was old and certainly not indigenous to its present location, its decoration evoking a gentrified past. In order to establish the provenance of this chamber organ, Texan organist and musicologist Dr. Susan Ferré did much scholarly research that, when coupled with a thorough restoration by Dr. Susan Tattershall, led her to assert that one of the first two St. Chrischona missionaries, Adam Sager, had brought this organ to Texas as a "gift from the St. Chrischona mission to Texas."[10] Constructed of walnut, oak, and pine, its manual compass is limited, but its 8 Gedackt, 8 Suavial, 4 Prestant, and 2⅔ Quint create a shimmering, undulating sound. A primitive and virtually inaudible pedal with only an "8 Bass" of open wood was crudely added to the instrument later. This instrument, which

---

9 *Choralbuch für die evangelische Kirche in Württemberg* (Stuttgart: Verlag der J. B. Metzler'schen Buchhandlung, 1876).

10 Susan Ferré, "Raising the Raisin Organ," *The Tracker*, Vol. 56, No. 2 (Spring 2006): 30–36. This fascinating organ deserves more attention than can be given here, but Ferré thoroughly documents the history of this instrument, and its mysteries, in this article.

previously had been housed at Trinity Lutheran Church in Victoria, Texas, and then later at Meyersville, Texas, is probably the first pipe organ of any type in the state. According to Ferré's and Tattershall's research, this organ from an unknown builder could date from as early as the eighteenth century, as suggested by "certain similarities to instruments of South German and Northern Swiss origin."[11]

To transport even a small chamber organ to the New World was no small feat, demonstrating the importance the first Lutheran pastors in Texas placed on music in the church, a fact not always discernable later in church and parish histories in Texas, which dedicate more historical discernment to the processes of parsonage building and the development of church social events than to general church practices, much less liturgical piety. Spittler himself, in establishing St. Chrischona in an extant but dilapidated Basel church building, had an organ built for the chapel in 1843, an indicator of his commitment to sacred music.[12] As St. Chrischona was and still is an ecumenical seminary, this is an important fact to note. If at times their orthodox Lutheran credentials were brought into question, particularly as they engaged with the nascent Missouri Synod in the state, there was certainly no Zwinglian liturgical aestheticism in the missionaries' spiritual formation. This little chamber organ demonstrates at minimum the importance these early missionaries placed on congregational singing. Spittler, in his canvasing for funds and matériel for the six additional missionaries he sent to Texas in 1851, explicitly states the need for *Kirchengesangbücher*, or hymnals, for the immigrants. Sager must have been musical himself, as the minutes from a synodical convention held in May 1859 at Meyersville, Texas, record that "Pastor Sager had brought along his organ from Victoria

---

11 Ibid.
12 Kober, *Christian Friedrich Spittler's Leben*, 167.

for the expressed delight of congregational singing."[13] Although
there is no way to document its actual liturgical application
when it arrived in Texas, the organ's presence does speak to the
intention of the St. Chrischona seminary to encourage singing
in the mission field. Certainly, congregational singing was no
afterthought to these Lutheran pioneers in Texas.

None of the preceding thumbnail history deals specifically
with the Lutheran Church–Missouri Synod (LCMS), whose
settlers had only begun to arrive in the United States in the
late 1830s, and even then established themselves only locally
elsewhere in the country. Texas history avoids a clean deline-
ation among the different Lutheran sects; immigrants would
align to whatever Texas iteration of the Lutheran Church from
their homeland was available to them, usually arranged along
national lines. The early Lutheran history of Texas is one of fluid-
ity, flexibility, and adaptation to a new environment, sometimes
with less concern for adherence to a particular denomination.
Additionally, with one exception that will be addressed subsequently, most of these earliest Lutheran pioneers in Texas were
motivated either by potential economic betterment as offered
by the land grants or by opportunities to escape the political travails of the revolutions of 1848 rather than by spiritual
concerns. Conversely, the founders of the Missouri Synod had
left the German lands motivated largely by a desire to worship freely, unhindered by the edicts of the Prussian Union of
Churches, which had attempted to reconcile theological differences between Lutherans and Reformed. With one exception,
the first St. Chrischona missionaries would align their congregations with the Texas Synod, a body associated first with the
old General Synod and then with the Iowa Synod. The exception was the aforementioned Rev. Braun, a founder of the First
Evangelical Synod of Texas who had established First Lutheran
Church in Houston. He would advise Salem Lutheran Church

---

13 Ferré, "Raising the Raisin Organ."

in Rose Hill, Texas (now Tomball), in 1871 to apply to the Missouri Synod for a pastor, and that congregation would become only the second LCMS congregation in the state.[14] While Braun was sympathetic and supportive of the Missouri Synod and was involved in the ordination of a new pastor at Rose Hill, he was only briefly rostered in the church. As a general principle, however, once founded, churches would join and leave the various synods as circumstances warranted. As insular as the LCMS could be, especially in the nineteenth century, the new congregations would have had to confront the existing liturgical and spiritual landscape that was so shaped by the St. Chrischona missionaries and the Texas Synod. This requires a reconstruction and examination of the liturgical terrain in this state, which considered its independence so paramount that Texans viewed themselves as part of neither the South nor the West. It was enough to be "Texas."

Singing God's Song in a Foreign Land

In November 1851, Rev. Philip Zizelmann, along with several other St. Chrischona missionaries, arrived in Texas, where, under the leadership of Rev. Braun, they participated in founding the first Evangelical Lutheran Synod of Texas only five days after their arrival. Within two weeks, after having sought discernment for their particular assignments, the pastors would go their separate ways, singing Count Zinzendorf's hymn "Jesus, Lead Thou On."[15] Zizelmann was charged with gathering a congregation in San Antonio, and in preparation, he surveyed the worship landscape of the locals, observing, "The type

---

14 Robert Koenig, *Pause to Ponder: A History of the Lutheran Church–Missouri Synod in Texas* (Austin: Texas District, LCMS, 1980): 4–5.

15 Willie Ann McColloch, "St. John's Lutheran Church, Ross Praire and Ellinger, Fayette County, Texas," Fayette County History, http://www.fayettecountyhistory.org/st_john_lutheran_intro.htm (accessed August 2, 2020).

of Catholicism is French, with the clergy themselves assigned from France. On Sundays, one can hear from the churches music of such noise with the banging of drums and the accompaniment of tambourines. —Of the Protestants, little good may be said. For the most part, their preaching pays off only in the secular world."[16]

This passage requires some interpretation. The first vicar apostolic of Texas (1841–47), Jean-Marie Odin, would subsequently be appointed bishop of Galveston (1847–61), under which the city of San Antonio was administered. France had early on recognized the new Republic of Texas, and Odin, born in France himself, worked tirelessly to evangelize Texas, eventually securing eighty-four priests from Europe, many from France, to serve the state.[17] Bishop Odin was no boorish populist. Zizelmann's evaluation displays prejudice against the liturgical music of the area, which certainly represents a culture shock from that to which he was accustomed, but certainly, the reality was more complex. By one account, Odin had an organ, probably a harmonium, installed in what was presumably his cathedral in Galveston. Odin's successor, Claude-Marie Dubuis, certainly had an organ (again, perhaps a reed organ) installed in Galveston; a Galveston journalist "passing the cathedral" in 1867 was "surprised to hear the organ played with a skill greater than we are accustomed to hear. We entered the church just in time to hear the conclusion of a mass. . . . We learned that the organist was a young Seminarian brought over by the Bishop on his last trip to Europe."[18] It does seem that the church music of the local Roman congregations, if simple and galling, was only so because it lacked

---

16 Mgebroff, *Ersten Deutschen*: 108.

17 Patrick Foley, "Odin, Jean Marie," Handbook of Texas Online, https://www.tshaonline.org/handbook/entries/odin-jean-marie (accessed September 13, 2020).

18 "Local Intelligence," *Flake's Weekly Galveston Bulletin* (December 25, 1867): 5.

resources rather than intent. Lutherans would confront the same scarcity of resources when they established their first churches too. Zizelmann's assessment of Protestant worship, while not mentioning anything of music, suggests that the preaching was either coldly rationalistic or perhaps evangelically heartwarming. Either way, the spiritual background of the Texans left much room for the Lutheran missionaries.

For most Lutheran congregations that associated with the Texas Synod during the 1850s and 1860s, worship must have been simple. Employing the Wollenweber Gesangbuch of the General Synod, churches were small, and if fortunate, singing would have been led by a harmonium, once the congregation could afford such a luxury. The historical record is particularly scant as to how congregational singing would actually have been performed.

The First Pipe Organs Built in Texas

Johann Traugott Wandke, like so many German immigrants of the time, arrived with his family in Galveston on the SS *Weser* on June 7, 1855, after which he would eventually settle in Round Top, Fayette County, Texas, where he built a stone house and workshop. The Prussian-born Wandke's journals reveal an organ builder of some training, although how thoroughly he was steeped in the art and with whom he apprenticed are unknown. The church building of Bethlehem Lutheran in Round Top was dedicated in 1866, although the organ was only completed in 1867. Wandke's organs were all constructed of native Texas materials, the suspended tracker instrument at Round Top utilizing cedar pipework, from which he would craft an 8 Gross Gedackt, 8 Viol di Gamba, 4 Viol di Gamba, 4 Klein Gedackt, 4 Principal, 2 Octave, 1½ Quinta, and 8 Trompete, plus Tremolo.[19] Gerald Frank summarizes the quality of workmanship of this organ:

> The difficulties in assessing the skill of the organ's builder are compounded by the fact that one must consider that Wandke was working under less-than-ideal circumstances. To have crafted all of the pipes by hand in a shop that was typical neither of pipe making nor of organ building shops, to have voiced all of the pipes from wood (which does not lend itself to the flexible maneuvering that makes metal pipes so much easier to voice), to have been apparently isolated in Texas from exposure to other pipe organs and organbuilders—all point to the stark independence into which Wandke was thrust in his work. That he was able to produce an instrument of the quality and refinement of the Round Top organ, one consistent with time-honored principles of organbuilding, indicates that he possessed more than an amateur's knowledge of and experience in organbuilding.[20]

Wandke's two other extant organs include an instrument of three ranks dating from 1863, certainly the oldest organ in Texas made completely in Texas, and another of four ranks, likely dating from 1868. This later instrument, with pipes constructed of pine, employs nomenclature with a decidedly English bent with its 8 Stopped Diapason, 4 Principal, 4 Flute, and an unnamed stop at 2 foot pitch. Frank's assessment of

---

19 Wandke's original Trompete has been replaced with an 8 Regal. According to Friedemann Buschbeck, who restored the organ in 2007, the Regal is a "replacement of the original Trompete 8 with wooden resonators at four foot length. But Wandke never finished the trumpet stop so it was unusable also by its construction and placement. During the restoration I replaced the Trompete with the 8 Regal to make this stop usable. The original reeds and resonators are now stored at the church." Buschbeck, personal correspondence with the author, January 15, 2022.

20 Gerald Frank, *A German Organbuilder on the Texas Frontier: The Life and Work of Johann Traugott Wandke* (Harrisville, NH: Boston Organ Club, 1990): 23.

Wandke insinuates what must have been a difficult life on the frontier:

> In every aspect of organbuilding Wandke demonstrated remarkable capability. The design of each of his three extant instruments shows a comfortable familiarity with classic organbuilding techniques. His organs are encased in the traditional manner. The layout of the chests conforms to normal practices. The key actions, pleasant to the touch, use stickers or suspended trackers. The wind systems support the sounds adequately. The pipes, taken as a whole, speak uniformly and musically.
>
> The uniqueness of his instruments lies primarily in their almost total construction of wood—the local native cedar for the most part, but also pine and maple (used perhaps only when, and because, it was available). That even some of the screws are hand-turned from cedar shows both the inventiveness of Wandke and the necessity of his "making do" with the best alternatives available to him.[21]

Wandke might not have been born in Texas, but his instruments represent the state's first "native" organ-building tradition, and a Lutheran one at that. The question might be proffered, however, as to how these organs were employed in the Lutheran service.

The Wandke *Choralbuch*

Among the many effects from Wandke's estate is an untitled *Choralbuch* manuscript that may or may not offer a glimpse of early Lutheran Texan hymn singing, but either way, it is one of the most significant volumes related to church music possessed by a Lutheran immigrant. *Choralbücher*, as a genre, provided organ accompaniments for the melodies in a particular hymnal. In this case, the music of the *Choralbuch* corresponds

---

21 Ibid.: 44–45.

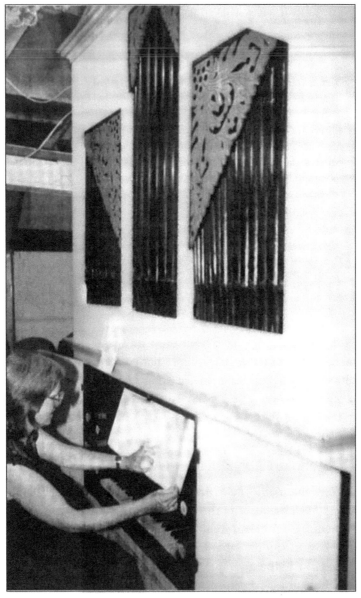

Figure 1.5 Susan Ferré at the Wandke organ at Bethlehem Lutheran, Round Top, Texas. (Source: Courtesy of Friedemann Buschbeck, who restored this instrument in 2007.)

to the hymns found in the *Sorauischen Gesangbuch*. Sorau, a Prussian province, was a region in Lower Lusatia bordering Silesia. Lutheran identity permeated this region. Now called Zary and located within the Polish border, even Georg Phillipp Telemann had spent a brief portion of his career in service of the court there. The *Sorauischen Gesangbuch* underwent a number of different editions, with each gaining new hymns. Wandke's *Choralbuch* contains 150 chorales, plus an alphabetical index to the hymns along with a "register" that provides cross-references to the *Gesangbuch*. These cross-references match the hymn numbering of the 1870 *Gesangbuch*, but not the 1807 edition. Since Wandke died in 1870, and he was living in Texas by then, this cannot be the corresponding edition. It is likely, then, that the *Choralbuch* corresponds to an 1841 version of the *Gesangbuch*. However, little more can be established of its provenance. Was it owned by Wandke or simply used by him, if indeed he served regularly as a church organist? Was it produced in Texas, or did Wandke or another immigrant bring it to the New World themselves? Certainly the German Texans had to confront the scarcity of musical resources in their new land. Could it have been composed here, thus reflecting the musical and liturgical vision the pioneers intended to establish in Texas?

The chorales in Wandke's *Choralbuch* are all presented isometrically, favoring the steadier, statelier rhythm of evened-out note values to the dance-like, sprightly rhythm exhibited in their sixteenth-century forebears. Isorhythmic chorales usually resulted in a generally slower tempo, and as such, each of the chorale accompaniments exhibits *Zwischenspielen*, those brief organ interludes between phrases that allow the congregation to breathe and to ponder the text. Hymn singing utilizing *Zwischenspielen* claims a long history in the Lutheran Church, as it was already a tradition in Bach's churches in Leipzig in the eighteenth century, and certainly represents a custom with

which many German Lutherans were familiar.[22] Most obviously, however, this style of hymn singing required an actual
keyboard to render. The German settlers in Texas initially
lacked organs, singing only a cappella, so this method of performance practice was rendered immediately obsolete. Does
Wandke's *Choralbuch* reflect a historical liturgical vision that
the Texas Lutherans sought to uphold but were only able to do
so after their congregations grew in affluence to afford organs?
Certainly, there is no record of hymn performance practice in
Texas that utilized *Zwischenspielen*, even later. The Wendish
Lutherans, originating from neighboring Upper Lusatia and in
Texas settling only thirty miles to the west of the Round Top
Lutherans, *did* produce a *Choralbuch* in 1872 that contains no
Zwischenspielen. At least by the time they had arrived in Texas,
that method of hymn performance practice had fallen into dis-
use in the Wendish community. If the congregation in Round
Top sang chorales using the *Zwischenspielen* per the *Choralbuch*, played on Wandke's 1867 pipe organ, it would not have
been a practice that could be easily translated to other Texas
contexts, lacking organs as they did.

Perhaps this dilemma encapsulates the reality of so much of
Texas Lutheranism in the nineteenth century, reflecting a desire
for certain ecclesiastical practices that were simply not possible
on the wilds of the prairies. Church buildings were eventually constructed, organs were built, and choirs were formed,
but these propitious moments occurred years after arrival and
after decades of enculturation. In that time, a community's
liturgical piety can change. After years of singing without an
organ and without those ubiquitous phrase interludes called
Zwischenspielen, will a church community wish to return to
the old manner of singing from perhaps an entire generation

---

22 See also Bach's "Allein Gott in der Höh' sei Ehr," BWV 715, which
   demonstrates how these organ interludes were integrated into the hymn
   singing.

Figure 1.6 "Jesus Meine Zuversicht" from the Wandke *Choralbuch*, demonstrating *Zwischenspielen* between each phrase. (Source: Courtesy of Dr. Gerald Frank.)

ago? The witness of modern people suggests this is not to be the case.

At the cornerstone-laying service for St. Paul Lutheran Church (Texas Synod) in 1883 in Cave Creek, Texas, the congregation sang that great Lutheran battle hymn "Nun Danket Alle Gott"; at the building dedication the next year, the guest choir from Zion Lutheran Church in Fredericksburg sang as an anthem "Vom Kirchlein im Thale," a German translation of the 1860s American gospel song "The Church in the Wildwood," no doubt acquired from the local Baptist or Methodist hymnal.[23] In terms of singing and hymnody, American culture relentlessly strove to pull the immigrants away from their spiritual roots, successfully enticing some strands of Lutheranism, particularly those founded by the early St. Chrischona missionaries, into the Texas Synod and into a more progressive liturgical mindset, while those associating with the nascent LCMS were more likely to retain their historic theology and liturgical practices.

---

23 *St. Paul Lutheran Church, Cave Creek, TX 1883–1983* (self-pub., 1983): 3.

2

Intertwining Fortunes

The First Lutheran Church–Missouri Synod Worship in Texas

The story of the LCMS in Texas must begin outside of both Texas and Missouri Synods, the narrative at times tending to complexity, beginning as it does with the Prussian and Saxon immigration to Texas. The first wave of immigrants arrived in Texas on December 16, 1854—some 460 Wendish souls whose venture into the New World was inspired by a desire for religious liberty and the freedom to practice their "Old Lutheran" faith, which the Prussian Union of Churches had challenged in their homeland of Upper Lusatia.[1] The Prussian Union, orchestrated by King Frederick William III in 1817, on the three hundredth anniversary of the Reformation, sought to unite Lutheran and Reformed congregations in Prussia through a single liturgy ("Agenda") that had been shorn of distinctive Lutheran theology. Numerous Lutheran congregations dissented against the forced edicts, motivating immigration to Australia and the United States, which surged in the 1840s. The Wends were the first group of Lutheran immigrants to Texas who were motivated primarily by the ideals of religious liberty rather than simply the enticement of

---

1 George R. Nielsen, *Johann Kilian, Pastor: A Wendish Lutheran in Germany and Texas* (Serbin: Texas Wendish Heritage Society, 2003): 44.

economic improvement, and their new colony at Serbin, in the lush post oak country of Central Texas, would exemplify both the struggles and successes of a colony ostensibly called and gathered around Lutheran preaching, the proper administration of the sacraments, and the practice of an Old Lutheran, Saxon liturgy, unencumbered by royal decrees or a rationalist hermeneutic. The Wends possessed a distinctive liturgical piety borne from the tension of centuries of living as Slavic Lutherans in German-speaking lands. This piety would transfer to Texas, as they would eventually become the first representatives of the LCMS in Texas, establishing the Wendish colony at Serbin, Texas, in 1854.

Jan Kilian as Pastor and Musician

Jan (Johann) Kilian, born in 1811 in Doehlen, in Saxony,[2] studied at Bautzen and at the University of Leipzig, where he possibly knew or met C. F. W. Walther, but with whose writings he was certainly acquainted. Before he accepted the call to shepherd the Wendish immigrants to Texas, he had served as pastor at Hochkirche, his home parish, after which he briefly continued his education at the Pilgermission St. Chrischona in Basel, Switzerland, an endeavor never fully realized, as he was subsequently called to the church at Kotitz after the death of his uncle, Rev. Michael Kilian, the previous pastor. In 1848, he began a pastorate at the Old Lutheran parishes of Weigersdorf and Klitten.[3]

Kilian was acquainted with matters of music and held firm opinions about the proper execution of the Lutheran liturgy. A prolific writer, during the late 1830s and throughout the 1840s he produced a constant stream of hymns and sacred poetry,

---

2 Ibid.: 1.

3 For a thorough account of these and others of Kilian's biographical particulars, see ibid.

Figure 2.1 The packet ship *Ben Nevis* in 1852 on an Australian run. The immigrant ship was owned by the company that in a later iteration would become the White Star Line. (Source: "Emigration to Australia: The 'Ben Nevis' Packet Ship," *Illustrated London News* [September 4, 1852]: 189.)

culminating in *Spěwarske wjesele* (*Joyful Singing*), a collection of poems first published in Bautzen in 1846.[4] Although there remains no record of his early musical education, he did achieve a state of higher musical proficiency, as he composed tunes for some of these texts in 1847. Although there is evidence that Kilian continued some compositional activity after his arrival in Texas, such creativity certainly would have been drastically reduced—the stresses of administering a parish in the Texas forests usurping his energy, a situation he would

---

4 Trudla Malinkowa, introduction to *The Poetry and Music of Jan Kilian*, ed. David Zersen (Austin, TX: Concordia University Press, 2010): 10. Although there are variations of the spelling of *Spěwarske* in the scholarly literature, this is the accepted presentation. The author's copy of Kilian's tune book from 1847 presents the title as *Spjewarske Weszelje*; however, according to Wendish language authority Weldon Mersiovsky, the orthography changed in 1948, rendering this an archaic spelling.

Figure 2.2 Rev. Jan Kilian. (Source: "Pfr. Johann Kilian," Ev.-Luth. Kirchgemeinde Hochkirch, https://www.kirche-hochkirch.de/neu/page54.html [accessed February 2, 2022].)

later lament. Kilian did consider himself a musician enough to guide the development of the sacred music of the Wendish in Texas. Of his own musical background, he wrote in 1869, "Incidentally, may I add that I am a musician, who can play every chorale, that I have worked through the 24 keys of music and am working on a Triad School which should serve for a faster training of good organists. One should bring me the best organist and musician that one has for my training. Neither should such a person be an arrogant musical idiot. I want to learn many things such as playing the pedals, from him."[5] Just how musically competent was Kilian? Lacking records to the contrary, the truth may be that he was only slightly more musically educated than the local "arrogant musical idiot" he wished to eschew. Perhaps he was sufficiently proficient in music to stay ahead of his organists, and there was certainly an organ in Serbin by 1860, the "young men" of the congregation having gathered $170 for an organ in conjunction with a new church building.[6] Certainly Kilian knew enough about organs, for as early as 1840, in a parish report for Kotitz, he expressed a desire that "instead of the Positive [organ] that had served as the organ, one could wish for a pedal organ."[7]

---

5 Johann Kilian, letter to Rev. G. A. Schieferdecker, June 28, 1869 (Concordia Historical Institute [CHI], Serbin Collection, 107.500). All references to this correspondence are from the online archive at the Wendish Research Exchange, https://forum.wendishresearch.org, which has been curated by Weldon Mersiovsky. Subsequent references to letters from the CHI, Blasig, or Weigersdorf collections are all found at this online archive under "Texas Wends: Letters and Documents."

6 Michael Buchhorn, ed., *A Collection of Histories of St. Paul Lutheran Church, Serbin, TX, in Commemoration of the Congregation's 150th Anniversary* (Serbin, TX: St. Paul Lutheran Church, 2003): 100.

7 Johann Kilian, "Kotitz," trans. Ed Bernthal, Wendish Research Exchange, https://forum.wendishresearch.org/viewthread.php?tid=3534 (accessed March 18, 2020). A "positive" organ is a small organ of one manual with perhaps one to four ranks of pipes. They were usually easily portable. Although functional, they lacked the tonal resources of larger organs.

Johann Carl Teinert, a farmer and fellow immigrant, had
helped gather a congregation of Old Lutherans together in
Dauben, Prussia, which ultimately resulted in the group's
immigration to Texas. He had served as organist and cantor
for Kilian in Europe and would reprise that role after settling in Texas. Indeed, Teinert may be considered the first
person to exercise the office of Lutheran cantor in Texas.
Five years Kilian's junior, Teinert served the new congregation at Serbin as organist, "song leader," and violinist. Kilian
writes of Teinert in one instance as one might describe a
self-trained organist:

> Carl Teinert . . . has the requirements that an organist and
> song leader in Serbin has to have, although he does not know
> the notes, so that nothing new can be brought in. And that is
> actually good, because the congregation does not love any-
> thing new, but wants to keep the old things that were brought
> here. And Teinert can do this. For this, the accomplished
> player that he is, under my supervision, he could learn the
> notes in almost four weeks if he could have an instrument
> in his home. But to complete the preparation for playing the
> organ, which the congregation especially requires, belongs to
> years of practice. But I don't have the knowledge of the note
> recognition and furthermore the proficiency in playing that
> Teinert has.[8]

Teinert, then, seemingly could play the chorales elegantly, but
perhaps his proficiency was borne through a good ear rather
than training. This is buttressed elsewhere when Kilian writes
that Teinert

> plays the organ nimbly even though he has forgotten the notes.
> He also plays the violin quite well. He previously learned the
> notes and the key and how they fit together. Now he does not

---

8 Johann Kilian, *Report on the Interviews with the Organists, Leubner and
Teinert*, June 6, 1869 (CHI, Serbin Collection, 106.867).

want to know anything about notes, but plays every melody that he can sing. And he is a good singer and sings most melodies. If a new melody is introduced, I play the notes for him until he knows them well enough to sing them. Then he plays them on the organ. Even an organ with pedals and many registers is not an embarrassment for him.[9]

It seems, then, that having "forgotten the notes" means that Teinert lacked the capacity to read a musical score, whether or not he indeed once had the capability to read music, as Kilian implies. Kilian treated Teinert as a professional. From 1860, Teinert was presented with an "unrestricted yearly harvest offering . . . brought for him on each Reformation festival," after which, in 1864, "he was assured of certain benefits for his organ playing and song leading at baptisms, weddings, and funerals and that he was to be paid by the Pastor, out of the church treasury, for his Sunday and Festival days expenses, a yearly sum of $10."[10] Kilian's appreciation for a cantor's appropriate remuneration is evidenced even from his days in Prussia, from where he described the equivalent position at Kotitz in 1837, at the time held by Johann Traugott Michalk: "The school master, as organist and sexton, received seven acres and pasture land, in addition to the incidentals for his church duties. He also received, in addition to the aforementioned benefits, an offering from the church. As school teacher he gets a yearly salary of $165 and 12 Reichstaler money for fuel."[11] And it was perhaps Kilian's notion of the *Kantoramt*, the office of the cantor, from which internecine controversy would emerge in the early days of the Texas Wends.

---

9 Johann Kilian, letter to J. W. Lindemann, June 26, 1868 (Texas Wendish Heritage Society Museum and Archives [TWHS], Blasig Collection, 102.500).

10 Kilian, *Report on the Interviews*.

11 Ibid.

Figure 2.3 Carl Teinert with his third wife, Anna Symmank. (Source: Texas Wendish Heritage Society Museum and Archives, photo #760.)

Jan Kilian had joined the LCMS in 1855, finding it a haven of orthodox practice relative to the unionism and unfettered pietism he perceived in the nascent Texas Synod, which had already enticed away other German immigrant groups. Yet the Serbin congregation itself had remained officially unaffiliated, possibly due to latent friction between the German and Wendish constituencies. The cultural differences between the Wends and the Germans in Prussia failed to moderate after the journey to Texas, and Kilian had to mitigate the tendencies for some in his congregation to form conventicles, or *Stunden*, the small groups so characteristic of the Pietist's *ecclesiola in ecclesia*. Initially, the Wendish element ran church business until the increasing numbers of German settlers required an administrative protocol in which both languages were used and both nationalities held ecclesiastical responsibilities. Yet this escalated the tension, and by 1859, a breakaway church calling itself St. Peter's, motivated by a propensity for Pietist practices and Methodist tendencies adopted from rather zealous local Protestant missionaries, established itself on the outskirts of Serbin, much to Kilian's chagrin. Although this church failed to prosper and would eventually reabsorb into the mother church in 1867, seeds of dissension had been sown that would manifest in the sacred music of the Wendish Lutherans.

Teacher Leubner and the Seeds of Conflict

The isolation of the Civil War had perhaps compelled the church in Serbin, now named St. Paul, to seek formal connections to a church body outside of Texas, preferably in the North, where the political settlers' sympathies had lain in the recent national conflict. Thus, St. Paul joined the LCMS in 1865, coveting, among other advantages, a process for calling subsequent pastors and teachers, Kilian himself complaining that his teaching in the parochial school had decreased the time he could devote to pastoral duties. Thus, after some political maneuvering for a few years in which the German, Wendish, and Pietist factions competed for power, the congregation would issue a call to a teacher from the synodical college, called a seminary, at Addison, Illinois, an institution reminiscent of the German *Gymnasium*, encompassing four years of secondary education and one year of college.[12] As was the custom for Lutheran teachers well into the twentieth century, synodical training endeavored to equip candidates not only to teach but to serve as church musicians for the community, usually playing the organ. Practically then as now, the music component certainly supplemented many a meager teacher salary, and thus was Ernst Leubner called as a teacher. At twenty-one years old, Teacher Leubner came from thoroughly German stock, a fact quite pleasing to the German faction in the parish. Professor Lindemann at Addison had recommended him highly in a June 1868 letter to Kilian:

> Ernst Leubner . . . is originally from Neugehrsdorf near Weigsdorf in Saxony (also in the vicinity of the beloved Kotitz). He is now 21 years old; he was in Brunn's Institute for five months, and a year with us. He is also about a year in America. We would not risk sending him out so soon, if we have not learned to know him as an honest, faithful, gifted, and diligent person. Of course all requests, which you find sketched in your letter, he does not match, nevertheless I must first ask, if you would have him, whether I in the other case send him forth immediately. He namely has knowledge of the English language and made a beginning with us on the piano, and has come so far with us, that we dare hope, that he himself can and would work out. He has made astounding progress in English, and even was the motivation that we determined him for you. We namely hope that he not only completely

---

12 Nielsen, *Johann Kilian*: 39.

appropriates English, but would also easily learn Wendish. He gives practice toward it.[13]

The terms of Leubner's call had been that he should learn Wendish and be able to play hymns in the Wendish fashion. That Teinert, a Wend, had been a cantor for Kilian both before and after his arrival in Texas should have given Kilian pause to consider the threat a new organist might bring to the community. Kilian did consider Teinert's situation, but in a letter to Professor J. W. Lindemann of the Addison seminary before Leubner's arrival, Kilian asserted that Teinert was "pleased with the vote [to call Leubner] because Mr. Leubner must first learn how to play organ. Teinert will gladly instruct him how to play the organ if he is willing to become a student."[14] Perhaps Kilian's paternal instincts clouded his judgment in the matter, as in the same letter, Kilian admits, "I am greatly concerned that he [Leubner] does nothing rash in response to my expressed wish in an earlier hurried letter that our teacher should enter into marriage. Therefore I am forced to explain that he, as a single man, will gladly be accepted and brought to us."[15] The Wendish pastor endured many sacrifices for this community and on behalf of orthodox Lutheranism, but by his own admission, he could be prone to "rash" comments and actions that served neither well. Therefore, with a call in hand to serve as a teacher and cantor at St. Paul, Teacher Leubner was installed on Sunday, August 30, 1868.[16]

Although Leubner was immediately installed as a teacher, his call as an organist and cantor seemed predicated on successfully demonstrating his ability first to conform to the local,

13 J. W. Lindemann, letter to Johann Kilian, June 4, 1868 (CHI, Serbin Collection, 101.600).

14 Kilian, *Report on the Interviews*.

15 Ibid.

16 Johann Kilian, sermon at Ernst Leubner's installation, August 30, 1868 (TWHS, Blasig Collection, 103.400).

Wendish, sacred music tradition, and with this, he seemed destined for failure. Whether he accepted the call with that particular understanding, the autumn of 1868 appeared to be a trial for his cantorship, wherein Kilian intended Leubner to learn service-playing duties from him and from Teinert, an apprenticeship only by the successful completion of which Leubner would be "installed" as the cantor. Extant historical sources represent only Kilian's views of the situation, so much interpretation is required. According to Kilian, Leubner's efforts as a cantor "did not totally please me at first. He seemed to have an inclination to neither Wendish or to music,"[17] although in evaluating him as a teacher, Kilian was free with his approbation, lauding him as "fresh, free, pious, happy and as a teacher, eager and energetic in general behavior."[18] Although Kilian only admits that Leubner "complained" about his situation that fall, one can imagine that Leubner would be irritated at the strictures of his bewildering apprenticeship under the two older men, neither of whom, at least to his perception, may have been as trained in music as he was. Within his first couple of months, a fever rendered Leubner bedridden, Kilian recalling, "He finally complained to me about his loneliness in such a high strung manner, that I thought best to take him to our house, until he again became healthy."[19] Kilian laments, however, Leubner's inability to learn Wendish service playing, observing metaphorically, "Concerning music, I have fished for him but have been unable to catch him. Early in this year [1869] he pledged to pursue music the Serbin way. Now he sees that he is rapidly moving toward his goal of learning our way. He had me teach him in the Teinert method. I was happy to do it."[20]

---

17 Johann Kilian, letter to J. W. Lindemann, February 8, 1869 (TWHS, Blasig Collection, 106.400).

18 Ibid.

19 Ibid.

20 Ibid.

Teinert continued playing services while, between teaching and harboring a fever, Leubner attempted to learn Wendish music. By November 1868, the congregation voted to confirm him as the organist, with the vote largely along ethnic lines, the Germans favoring his moving forward in the post, while the Wends were notably ambivalent. Kilian remained officially neutral but apparently did not consider Leubner's training complete, as he wrote in February 1869 that Leubner had only "played the organ twice for the German service. The first time Teinert went to see if Leubner had the courage. And it was satisfactory. Several false notes betrayed his being German. The Serbin music school interests him. He often listens to me how I play the hymn melodies without notes in each chosen key and how well I can play chorales set down on a sheet."[21] Leubner must have been granted organ-playing duties in March or April 1869, as by Easter of that year, Teinert had refused to play, relinquishing his duties to the young organist whose abilities at Wendish performance practice were far inferior to his own. By June, the conflict between the two organists worsened, no doubt aggrieved by Kilian's confusing management of the situation and by the congregation's gradual realization that the conflict evidenced the deeper rift between the adherents of the German language and those of the Wendish. The two organists served as pawns in a struggle between languages, cultures, and even ethnicities.

Teinert next forced a congregational vote in June 1869, the business of which was to confirm his own call as the organist, which indeed the congregation voted to do. Enraged, the young Leubner protested for installation into a call that was rightly his. Kilian agreed that Leubner's assignment is to "take over the responsibilities and punctually serve as the Cantor, to play the organ, and, under the supervision of the Pastor, to learn the local way of singing the hymns. But since the congregation in

---

21 Ibid.

Serbin consists of mostly Wends and its worship services are conducted not only in German, but for now primarily in the Wendish language, so it is imperative that the called teacher to be able to carry out the service of the Cantor, would learn to read the Wendish hymns and collects."[22] Yet in the *Report on the Interviews with the Organists, Leubner and Teinert* of June 6, 1869, Kilian continues, "Mr. Leubner has now been called to serve as the Cantor in Serbin. No one will deny him this call. But he cannot be installed into the office of Cantor to which he has been called, before he can play our church hymns we use in an orderly way, and to lead the singing. The Pastor requires, especially for the Holy Communion and for funerals, to have a song leader who can properly lead the Wendish hymns."[23] Kilian reaffirms that Leubner is not yet fit to discharge his call properly, as "his progress in Wendish is still insufficient that he could be in a position to lead the singing for funerals and communion. Also, he has now only learned several of the easier melodies, how these, according to our customary ways, are to be sung. Therefore, Mr. Leubner cannot yet be installed into the office of Cantor, even though he has been called to it. The actual installation to this office can follow only after he is in a position to completely fulfill all the duties of the office."[24] The Wends sang the Lutheran chorales isometrically—that is, with the uniform note values inherited from the time of Bach rather than the energetic, buoyant rhythms of the original melodies. The Germans largely knew and preferred the original melodies, tunes that, for example, C. F. W. Walther had so diligently taught in his *Singstunde* for the churches in St. Louis.[25]

---

22 Kilian, *Report on the Interviews.*

23 Ibid.

24 Ibid.

25 Although certainly the German immigrants would have had no connection to the St. Louis Germans—they would have known these hymn versions from their homeland. And even so, the case must not be overstated,

Certainly, Kilian realized the issue was primarily one of cultural conflict, yet perhaps he felt that addressing the manner in which the hymns were sung would assuage at least his Wendish detractors. To that end, he redoubled his study of the "musical tone arts" so as to arrange the hymn melodies as they were sung by the Wends at Serbin. In a letter to Rev. Caspar Braun in Houston in April 1869, Kilian asserts, "I have studied music industriously now since Leubner has been here, and have written down many chorales the way they are sung by the Wends."[26] This *Choralbuch* would be completed in 1872, much too late to abet the current feud. Customarily, a *Choralbuch* contains the four-part arrangements of each tune in a particular hymnal, arranged generally for organ accompaniment but also suitable for four-part singing. (Although generally, *Choralbücher* contained no hymn texts.) It seems that no *Choralbuch* had traveled with the Wends to Texas, as Teinert seemed mostly to play what he already knew by ear, and Leubner had difficulty learning new tunes. Playing the hymns in a Wendish manner cannot have represented an unreasonable demand for Leubner if he had had music to read; however, the magnitude of the order of difficulty is greatly enhanced if Leubner were expected to absorb, by ear, the pastor's playing or singing of new versions of chorale tunes he was already accustomed to playing another way. Learning to play back an original melody presents difficulties, but learning a chorale one *already knows*, incorporating manifold minuscule melodic and harmonic alterations, requires an altogether different level of sophistication that Leubner had yet to develop. Perhaps Kilian failed to realize exactly what he was asking Leubner to do.

---

as the readoption of the rhythmic chorale in Europe was a slow process throughout the nineteenth century.

26 Johann Kilian, letter to Rev. Caspar Braun, April 19, 1869 (TWHS, Blasig Collection, 106.800).

A Conflict Deepens

The conflict between the two organists taxed Kilian's diplo-
matic skills, although one strains to sympathize with Kilian,
as his own mismanagement of the situation led to its infe-
licitous outcome. Kilian attempted a maneuver of the via
media, acknowledging to the congregation that he had "urged
Mr. Leubner to play the organ." He continued, "But I encouraged him to play the organ, not as the Pastor in the name of the
congregation, or considered him to be the installed organist,
but only as a musician that he would get into the practice." One
cannot help but feel sympathy toward poor Leubner, who had
been called as an organist and cantor only to find he would not
be permitted to exercise those calls. Kilian *may* have grasped
the theological nuances and practical application of how to
utilize a noninstalled, but called, worker for an indeterminate
amount of time, but such theological niceties certainly had not
been made transparent to his resident farmer cantor, or to his
new twenty-one-year-old teacher, whose advanced education
probably amounted to no more than two years of college and
perhaps one year of piano.[27] Kilian concludes the matter, at
least in his own mind, hoping for peace but surely knowing the
animosity potentially engendered by such a nondecision:

> Therefore, my view now is this: That the doubts about Carl
> Teinert's position should herewith be lifted from the congre-
> gation, regarding his serving as Cantor, and that the authority
> that he had up to now over the organ, should be an official
> declaration, be confirmed as long as Mr. Leubner has not fully
> achieved the responsibility for the office of Cantor to which
> he has been called, and to which he cannot yet be installed or
> inducted. And what belongs to the use of the organ, I place
> myself under Teinert, and Mr. Leubner places himself under
> the Pastor. All questions, regarding the proposed relationship,

---

27 George R. Nielsen, "Wendish Leaders," *Texas Wendish Heritage Society
and Museum Newsletter*, Vol. 17, No. 1 (January 2004): 6–8.

that some might have, he should tell me, and I will talk to Teinert, as my superior, about it. But from both, the Pastor asks for humility and patience.[28]

No mention is made in the historical record of whether Leubner received payment for his musical services during this "apprentice" stage for his cantorial duties, but one can reasonably assume remuneration was intended to be withheld until his installation. If Leubner knew nothing of this arrangement until his arrival in Serbin, one can sympathize with his anger and sour disposition. Although Kilian had in 1866 called a pastor/teacher from Missouri to assist with the school—an experiment that also ended poorly—Kilian's experience in calling a teacher/cantor was limited. Perhaps he expected a level of musical sophistication that was unreasonable given the candidate's age, training, background (thoroughly German), and experience.

Kilian's "Resolution"

Nonetheless, in April 1870, Kilian declared the controversy of the cantorship "resolved," declaring, "[Teinert] alternates playing and singing with Leubner, who in organ playing has achieved so much in such a short time, that I am awe struck. What could this energetic man become if he were humble? In accordance with the written agreement executed this year on February 14 Leubner and the old organist, Carl Teinert, divided the responsibilities of the cantor position."[29] Yet Kilian presciently, if reluctantly, could discern that musical issues were simply a bellwether for more significant rifts in his congregation. In a letter to C. F. W. Walther in April 1870, Kilian

---

28 Kilian, *Report on the Interviews*.
29 Johann Kilian, letter to C. F. W. Walther, April 4, 1870 (CHI, Serbin Collection, 110.500).

observed, "In the fight over the administration of the office of cantor and of the school the conflict between things Wendish and things German also entered the discussion. Yet also this fight over the proportion of both nationalities is dominant if not on the whole of cardinal importance."[30] The struggle was about more than singing rhythmic or isometric melodies; these intense disagreements rather emanated from two deeply held national identities.

In the meantime, the influx of new residents in Serbin's Lee County and the strong cotton market after the Civil War resulted in prosperity to the congregation. A new stone building with double balconies and elevated pulpit, reminiscent of the churches they knew from Upper Lusatia, was begun in 1867, but only finished in 1871, delayed partly due to congregational conflict. Nonetheless, Kilian wanted the finest organ that could practically be installed, to which end he ordered, under Teinert's direction, a $200, nineteen-register harmonium with pedals from Phil. J. Trayser in Stuttgart, arriving in the spring of 1869.[31] Kilian would finally have an organ with pedals, a desire he had nurtured since his report about the Positive instrument in Kotitz, and Teinert would have an organ that he could handle with "no embarrassment." Yet peace was not to be.

Disagreement among the three men, certainly aggravated by their supporting factions, resulted in another chaotic congregational meeting on May 22, 1870, in which, although the details are sparse, Kilian himself resigned from his pastorate. Leubner then "claimed the school for his faction, denying Kilian the use thereof."[32] The congregation indeed split—not even the first time in the church's short history, but on June 12,

---

30 Ibid.
31 Johann Kilian, letter to Messrs. J. Kaufmann & Co., March 20, 1869 (TWHS, Blasig Collection, 106.700).
32 Arthur C. Repp, "St. Paul's and St. Peter's Lutheran Churches, Serbin, Texas, 1855–1905," *Concordia Historical Institute Quarterly*, Vol. 16, No. 1 (April 1943): 18–28.

Figure 2.4 St. Paul Lutheran in Serbin completed its stone church building in 1871. (Source: Texas Wendish Heritage Society Museum and Archives, photo #465.)

Kilian's supporters extended him a call to continue pastoring their party. A new congregation, called again St. Peter's, absconding with about a third of the members, was established in Serbin, only a few hundred feet away from the mother church. Leubner would teach at St. Peter's, and Kilian would return to teaching the school associated with the original St. Paul, although his dissatisfaction with his lot increased, and he continued to seek that elusive call north.

A Coda for Leubner and Teinert

Ernst Leubner's subsequent life can only be ascertained from a vague description in his obituary in the *Austin Daily Statesman* from August 1910: "Mr. Leubner was 63 years old and was one of the pioneer settlers of Serbin, having taught one of the first schools at that place. He had taught school for the past forty years in several states, was manager of several orphan homes in different states and was well known and liked by everybody.

He leaves a widow, brother and other relatives."[33] His obituary in the *Houston Post* further observed that his funeral "was attended by one of the largest gatherings seen at a funeral at Serbin in many years."[34] It is perhaps telling, and indicative of grace and reconciliation, that Jan Kilian's son Hermann, then pastor at St. Paul, Serbin, officiated. Another Kilian son and the present teacher at the St. Paul School, Gerhard, served as a pallbearer.[35]

Kilian's "resolution" was at least as pleasing to Teinert as it was to Leubner. In November 1871, during a congregational meeting in which plans were being formulated for the dedication of the new stone church, Teinert, who lived several miles south of Serbin, at Rabbs Creek, suggested that a new school be established in that area as a matter of convenience for the residents. Kilian saw this maneuver as an affront from Teinert, simply meant to embarrass Kilian. Nonetheless, this faction, led by Teinert, organized a "school congregation" called New Start.[36] The restive rebels soon clamored for their own Sunday congregation, arguing that "mules did not get any rest even on Sundays since they had to draw the entire family great distances to church. They felt that this was unscriptural, for even the beasts should be given rest."[37] Thus, in 1873, members from both St. Peter's and St. Paul formed their own congregation, called Holy Cross, under the leadership of Teinert and based at Rabbs Creek. Although Kilian had not given his blessing, the LCMS sent a pastor to the new church, further irritating Kilian. Although Teinert's reasoning for establishing a new congregation on the outskirts of the parish was sound, it is hard to imagine his motives were completely altruistic, and Kilian himself,

---

33 "Professor E. Leubner," *Austin Daily Statesman* (August 4, 1910): 3.

34 "Ernst Leubner Dead: Was Prominent in Educational and Church Circles at Giddings," *Houston Post* (August 7, 1910): 3.

35 Ibid.

36 Buchhorn, *Collection of Histories*: 112.

37 Ibid.: 113.

Figure 2.5 Ernst Leubner, the first Lutheran teacher in Texas, and the aspiring second Lutheran cantor in Texas. (Source: Texas Wendish Heritage Society Museum and Archives, photo #445.)

who had hoped to unify the Wendish people in one church and community in Texas, impractical as that vision may have been, was distressed and wounded in spirit.

As for Teinert, he served as the organist and cantor at Holy Cross, which, in 1875, "purchased a melodeon, a small

Figure 2.6 Ernst Leubner and his wife, Anna. (Source: Texas Wendish Heritage Society Museum and Archives, photo #430.)

reed organ, from Mr. Urban in Giddings."[38] Interestingly, as the school began to call teachers and the community grew, Teinert seemingly rotated out of his cantorial duties, relinquishing them first to a Mr. Kasper in 1877 and subsequently to Teacher Regner, who resigned in 1886, after which Teinert again resumed his organist duties. Whether these transitions from Teinert to others, including a called teacher, went more smoothly than they had with Leubner at Serbin, the records do not indicate, but it was clearly a pattern with which Teinert was familiar. Presumably, Teinert was instrumental in the purchase of the church's first pipe organ, as he had been with Serbin's Trayser harmonium almost two decades prior, when J. G. Pfeffer of St. Louis, Missouri, installed an organ at Holy Cross in 1892, the first pipe organ in an LCMS church in Texas. The old organ was given to the newly formed Trinity Lutheran in La Grange.[39] Johann Carl Teinert outlived two of his three wives, and according to historian Dr. George Nielsen, Teinert had "left a legacy, not only of his nineteen children, but three congregations which he helped to establish, two in Texas and one in Prussia."[40] Teinert died in 1904 at age eighty-four and was buried in the cemetery at Holy Cross, Warda.

Wendish Liturgical Praxis

While a comprehensive reconstruction of Jan Kilian's liturgical theology is outside the scope of this study, his personal spiritual and liturgical formation certainly shaped Wendish life in Texas, most notably as it was manifest in public worship. Scholar Trudla Malinkowa asserts that "Kilian is a singer of the Lutheran Awakening movement of the 19th century,

38 *125 Years of God's Grace: 1873–1998 Holy Cross Lutheran Church, Warda, TX* (Warda, TX: Holy Cross Lutheran Church, 1998): 84.
39 Ibid.
40 Nielsen, "Wendish Leaders": 6–8.

which unifies in itself the pietism and orthodoxy of the 18th century."[41] Stepping back from Kilian specifically, the Wendish Old Lutheran theological worldview must be considered when evaluating their sacred music in Texas, for this spirituality was informed by the tension arising from a life within these twin strands of Lutheran orthodoxy and pietism. It is helpful to state that the Wends were not a monolithic culture more so than any other is; the Wendish language, for example, is divided into Upper and Lower Sorbian, of which the Texas Wends were mostly Upper Sorbian–speaking. Yet some theological generalizations are fair considering the small size of their homeland, situated within modern Germany and Poland, specifically within the states of Saxony and Prussia, with sections historically in the Lands of the Bohemian Crown, later becoming part of the Kingdom of Prussia. Further, if the Texas Wends were unified in their desire to find a land where they could practice religious freedom, they still had difficulty finding a unified vision as to how to work out their theology in a societal context, to which their numerous factions and rogue church establishments attest.

Theirs was a conservative worldview, adhering to the "Old Lutheran" symbolical books, preaching, liturgy, and hymns, which had been threatened by the Prussian Union and corresponding worship restrictions in Saxony. As a young man with more free time, Kilian had labored to translate into Wendish important documents of the Lutheran faith, representing hundreds of years of tradition. From Luther's *Small Catechism* to the *Book of Concord* and many of the chorales translated into Wendish, Kilian's interest was in preserving the Lutheran faith unencumbered by rationalism or any other theological novelty of the prior century. The Prussian Union had sought to minimize theological differences between Lutheran and Reformed, instilling in the Wendish Texans an abiding mistrust for any

---

41 Zersen, *Poetry and Music*: 10.

sort of unionism. Thus the Texas Synod, with its syncretic tendencies, held little appeal for most of them and simply revolted Kilian. Motivated by a desire for missionary work, he had briefly attended the Pilgermission St. Chrischona in 1837, from where most of the other Lutheran missionaries in Texas had been sent, but forsook further study there because "the unionistic nature of the Basel mission school prevented [him] from carrying out [his] plan."[42] The Old Lutherans rejected liturgies that were not distinctly Lutheran, preferring a more historic model, as Kilian explains in a letter to C. F. W. Walther in 1858: "I also feel a dislike for a church service that is so barren, almost without liturgy, as it here appears. The old Saxon style and manner in which the church service and sacraments are held has gone over into my flesh and blood. And I know that the Missouri Synod upholds for all practical purposes, my churchly mentality."[43] Not only did Kilian prefer the traditional Saxon liturgy; he preferred hymnals with few novelties or innovations, writing in 1840 of the church at Kotitz that "a special blessing for Kotitz is the fact that no new style, watered-down hymnal has been introduced here."[44] Although Kilian's personal piety would shape the Wendish communities in Texas, his congregation of Wends and increasing numbers of Germans frequently countered his ideas with their own, hence the acrimonious founding of the dissident churches around Serbin.

One characteristic of Pietism, the formation of conventicles (*Stundenchristen*), or small groups organized by laity for spiritual devotions, had been a characteristic of many of the Old Lutherans who had sought relief from the state churches in Prussia and Saxony. In Prussian regions, the Wendish Lutherans

---

42 Johann Kilian, letter to Adolph von Harless, November 24, 1851 (Weigersdorf Archive as found at https://forum.wendishresearch.org/, 014.000).

43 Johann Kilian to C. F. W. Walther, March 13, 1858 (CHI, Serbin Collection, 034.500).

44 Kilian, "Kotitz."

had been most concerned by the new liturgy that, among other matters, altered the Words of Institution in the Eucharist. The Prussians departed from the state church in order to preserve their Eucharistic liturgy, administered by a properly ordained celebrant, establishing independent congregations. Although the independent churches were still constricted in some ways and forfeited state funding, they were able to receive properly administered communion in public together. About three hundred Prussians would immigrate to Texas. The situation differed just over the border in Saxony, where the proper liturgy was maintained and the Eucharist properly administered, but where the preaching had become inculcated with rationalist thought, and moralism and righteous living subsumed preaching of the gospel. The Saxons, then, remained in their churches to receive communion but met in small groups during the week, usually led by laity, to discuss the Scriptures and confessional books, to pray, and to sing traditional hymns.[45] Such conventicles would be difficult to abandon for the approximately two hundred Saxons who would follow Kilian to Serbin.[46]

The immigrants carried their social baggage to the New World. Scholar George Nielsen maintains that "in Europe the people of the conventicle movement had supported Kilian, but in Texas the meetings became the hotbed of opposition. The Saxons criticized Prussians for their withdrawal from the State church, and Kilian and the Prussians faulted the Saxons for their insistence on prayer meetings as a sign of a living faith. Both segments agreed on the essentials, however, and that basis was the Lutheran confessions."[47] Conventicle movements are generally characterized by emotionalism and a concern

---

45 Nielsen, *Johann Kilian*: 20–23.

46 For a detailed contrast of Prussian and Saxon theological concerns, see George R. Nielsen, "Prussian or Saxon: Part 2," Texas Wendish, July 1, 2015, https://texaswendish.org/2015/07/01/prussian-or-saxon-part-2/ (accessed July 19, 2020).

47 Nielsen, *Johann Kilian*: 53.

for visible "fruits of the Spirit," and they are less concerned with structured, public worship and the theological niceties as embodied in the Lutheran symbolical books. Indeed, the Serbin "conventicleists asked for a devotional format and firm application of church discipline, while the opponents favored a formal church service and argued that such discipline would not result in better, more Christian lives."[48] Yet even in Serbin, "Some Prussians . . . supported the conventicles and many Saxons favored a liturgical service."[49] This tension in liturgical praxis would permeate worship life throughout the elder Kilian's tenure as pastor.

The Wendish *Choralbuch* (1872)

Returning to the tribulations in Serbin of 1870, in the midst of the turmoil between Leubner and Teinert, Kilian found solace in shaping the vocational development of his own son. Gerhard August Kilian was born in 1852, the only one of the four children born in Europe to Jan Kilian and his wife, Maria, to survive into adulthood. In 1867, Gerhard had begun studies at Concordia Teachers Seminary in Addison, Illinois, where, in the autumn of 1870, he would continue with a two-year program of advanced study. Gerhard was in the process of learning to play the organ, as Kilian writes in the autumn of 1870 that Gerhard "played the new organ at church here one time. This was his first attempt at playing in public. His playing was more pleasing than Leubner's."[50] Two years later, Kilian would affirm even more pleasure in his son's progress, observing, "My son is performing well. He plays the organ so well that I must express my satisfaction with the teaching of music at the seminary in Addison. Especially

48 Ibid.: 54.
49 Ibid.: 53.
50 Johann Kilian, letter to Rev. Caspar Braun, October 4, 1870 (TWHS, Blasig Collection, 111.000).

do I like how Gerhard plays the pedals." The music instruction at Addison, the forerunner of Concordia University Chicago, must have so pleased Kilian that he sent Gerhard to complete a project that, if finished years earlier, would have saved the older man much heartache and stress. This project is manifest in a fair copy manuscript of Wendish hymns entitled *Choralbuch für evangel. luth. Gemeinde in Serbin, Texas.*[51]

This *Choralbuch* documents Wendish hymn singing and performance practices, differing as they did from standard German practices, giving practical insights into what actually constituted that elusive Wendish manner of singing. The large, oblong-shaped *Choralbuch* contains 240 four-part chorales intended for an organist to play and was carefully and beautifully calligraphed by a certain "Richard Gerstenberger, Addison," who signed it both on the title page and at the end.[52] The manuscript contains copious notes, from rubrics, to performance instructions, to sources, to reference materials, to other simple descriptors. The handwriting does not appear to be Kilian's. Gerhard, as the new cantor in 1872, could have executed all or some of the notations under the supervision of his father. The chorales have no associated hymn texts copied with them, so they were clearly not intended for ensemble choral singing. An *Anhang*, or supplementary material, is composed of a four-part motet by Jan Kilian, followed by an index and then a "Wendisch Litanie, 396," a musical setting that appears to be from

---

51 Jan Kilian, ed., *Choralbuch für evangel. luth. Gemeinde in Serbin, Texas* (n.p., 1872). This handwritten manuscript is kept at the Texas Wendish Heritage Society Museum and Archives in Serbin.

52 There is a Richard Gerstenberger active as an organist, pianist, and music teacher in Kansas, working for Pomeroy and Meads music store in Wichita, in the 1870s. According to an advertisement in the *Wichita Weekly Beacon* of November 5, 1879, "Piano and organ thoroughly taught and principle lessons in German given at moderate rates by Rich. Gerstenberger, teacher and organist" (3). There is nothing in this description that would not fit the profile of Gerhard's friend and scribe in Addison.

Figure 2.7 Gerhard Kilian. (Source: Texas Wendish Heritage Society Museum and Archives, photo #159.)

yet another hand. Three additional four-part motets, written in a different ink and certainly by a different scribe, complete the manuscript. In April 1869, Kilian mentioned that he had begun writing down the chorales in the Wendish manner, of which this manuscript certainly is the ultimate fulfillment of that need.[53] Although the historical record indicates nothing

53 Kilian, letter to Braun, April 19, 1869.

Figure 2.8 The Serbin *Choralbuch*. (Source: Texas Wendish Heritage Society Museum and Archives, photo taken by the author.)

more of the manuscript's genesis, it seems likely that Kilian sent his draft to Addison with Gerhard, where Gerstenberger must have been commissioned to complete the fair copy. The only firm date, by Gerstenberger's signature above the motet, is "Addison, June, 1872," so the entire manuscript must have been completed immediately before Gerhard's final return home, as he was installed as a teacher in Serbin that September. The volume represents the first and oldest surviving example of a *Choralbuch* for an LCMS congregation in Texas.

The *Choralbuch* was intended as a companion volume to the official hymnal of the Upper Lusatian States, *Duchowne kěrlišowe knihi*, known in the German colloquial as the *Wendische Gesangbuch* (*WG*).[54] First compiled by Jan Gotthelf Böhmer in Bautzen and published in 1741, this hymnal was the first

---

54 Jan Gotthelf Böhmer, *Duchowne kěrlišowe knihi* (Bautzen, 1741).

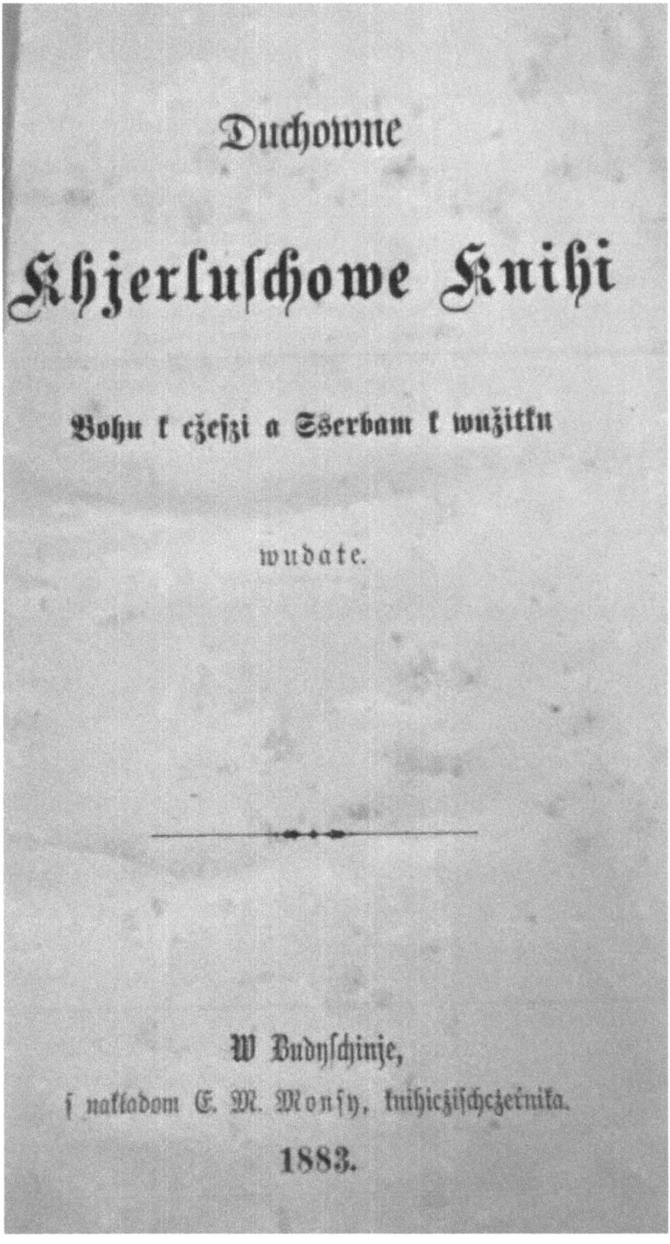

Duchowne

Khjerluschowe Knihi

Bohu k cżeści a Sserbam k wużitku

wudate.

———•◆•———

W Budyschinje,
s nakładom E. M. Monsy, knihicżischcżernika.

1883.

Figure 2.9 The Wendish hymnal. (Source: Provided by the author.)

to contain only texts in the Upper Sorbian language rather than including German versions on facing pages. The 1741 version contained 529 hymns, plus a concluding section of prayers. Between 1741 and 1909, about thirty editions of the hymnal were printed, with each successive iteration containing successively more hymns than the former.[55] By 1874, the book already included 816 hymns, but Kilian's reference numbers only reach 632, so his personal copy would have been a significantly earlier edition. This was certainly the primary hymnal in use at Serbin during the early years, at least when most of the inhabitants were indeed Wendish speaking, before the influx of German speakers by the early 1860s, who likely brought along their own *Gesangbücher* and might have had access to the hymnal of the LCMS, the 1847 *Kirchengesangbuch für Evangelisch-Lutherische Gemeinden ungeaenderter Augsburgischer Confession*. In a June 26, 1868, letter to Professor Lindemann in Addison, Kilian indicates that some in the community used the LCMS hymnal: "I would also like to suggest that he [Leubner] bring with him a small stock of books that he might need. . . . For example, there are no copies of the St. Louis hymn books here anymore. . . . The large print edition of the St. Louis hymnal is best. The middle print is acceptable. But the small print is not favored."[56] One interpretation of this may be that Kilian himself distributed this hymnal to parish families. Indeed, that there were "no copies" left probably means he had distributed all in his possession, which he presumably intended to do with any more that would come his way. This hymnal had its own accompaniment editions, initially utilizing Friedrich Layritz's settings, which differed significantly from the Wendish book.

---

55 Gerald Stone, "The Sorbian Hymn," trans. Weldon Mersiovsky, in *Perspektiven sorbischer Literatur*, ed. W. Koschmal (Cologne, Germany: Böhlau, 1993): 79–95, available at https://wendishresearch.org/2017/09/20/the-sorbian-hymn/ (accessed August 1, 2020).

56 Kilian, letter to Lindemann, June 26, 1868.

Music

According to an annotation in the manuscript, the musical settings of the hymns are taken from two principle sources, the first being the *Choralmelodien zu dem wendischen Gesangbuch* (Bautzen, 1858), edited by Carl Eduard Hering. Hering, born in 1807 in Saxony and dying in 1879 in Bautzen, was a minor composer whose chief claim to renown lies in his correspondence with Felix Mendelssohn and Robert Schumann.[57] The second source volume is the *Vollständiges Choralbuch zum Zwickauer Gesangbuch* (Zwickau: Zückler, 1865), although it was properly titled *Vollständiges Choralbuch zum Zwickauer sowie auch zum Dresdner und Leipziger Gesangbuch*, arranged by Karl Emanuel Klitzsch, a cantor at Zwickau, noted composer, correspondent with Schumann, and fairly prominent music critic of the late nineteenth century who contributed to the monumental music periodical *Neue Zeitschrift für Musik*.[58]

Returning to the Wendish *Choralbuch*, tunes are arranged isometrically, meaning the rugged, energetic rhythms of the original versions have been evened out whereby the fewest note values as possible are employed. The quarter value, with an occasional eighth note decoration, predominates, and hymn tempi could easily tend toward the lugubrious. In the United States, these versions of the chorale were preferred by most immigrant groups, including the Scandinavian Lutherans and the Germans whose settling in the country was not connected with the Saxon exodus that resulted in the formation of the LCMS. The usage of isometric chorale tunes was by no means unusual with Lutherans in the nineteenth century; these versions had predominated at least since Bach's time, whose settings generally utilized the chorale isometrically. This is in keeping with the Wendish spirit

---

57 Alfred Baumgartner, *Music der Romantik* (Salzburg, Austria: Kiesel, 1983): 290.

58 Waldo Selden Pratt, *The History of Music: A Handbook and Guide for Students* (New York: G. Schirmer, 1907): 512.

of conservatism and eschewing innovation—despite the fact
that isometric tunes were themselves a later innovative development from the originals. Consider the famous "Ein feste Burg"
("A Mighty Fortress") from the Serbin *Choralbuch*:

Figure 2.10 "Ein feste Burg," #127 in the *Choralbuch*. (Source:
Provided by the author.)

Although it would have been likely that the ends of phrases
would have been treated with a fermata and held longer by the
congregation, this entire melody demonstrates only two note
values—long and short—and most of them are the quarter
note long values. There are no time signatures throughout, and
bar lines are employed simply to divide the phrase in half. The
first two measures before the repeat are essentially 8/4, while
the remaining measures are set in 6/4, except for the final bar,
which reverts to 8/4. In essence, bar lines here indicate nothing of rhythm; they are simply a means of visually arranging
the music on the page. In fact, in some chorales, the placement
of the bar line seems arbitrary, with random "bars" of odd-
numbered beats having little to do with the meter of the tune.

Figure 2.11 "Wir Glauben," #5, notably uses the eighteenth-century
tune rather than the chant tune. This strict 4/4 time hymn begins

on a weak beat (beat 2), but there is no such indication here. Read literally, the first chord here is weak, and the second is strong, which was certainly not how it was originally composed or likely sung in practice. The Wendish tradition relied on an aural preservation of these melodies, the exact notation of which was of less importance. (Source: Provided by the author.)

This practice could also result in slower tempi, as the organist might have more difficulty visualizing, and thus internalizing, the strong/weak pattern. Yet this is all consistent with common practices in contemporary hymnals of the era. Consider this same hymn from a *Choralbuch* compiled by August Ritter for the province of Brandenburg, published in 1859:[59]

Figure 2.12 A. G. Ritter, "Ein feste Burg." (Source: A. G. Ritter, ed., *Choral-Buch zu den in der Provinz Brandenburg gebräuchlichen Gesangbüchern, Op. 36* [Erfurt, Germany: Gottfhilf Wilhelm Körners Verlag, 1859]: hymn 95, available at Deutsche Digitale Bibliothek, https://www.deutsche-digitale-bibliothek.de/item/ 4Q26MAUSNBCX7AUSFPPVBALYX2C52XXG [accessed January 18, 2022].)

Although Ritter's version conveys the stately nature of the isometric chorale, even this version is a bit more adventurous than the Wendish version. Consider the Wendish third "measure" versus the Ritter fifth measure—the melody is adapted whereby

59 A. G. Ritter, ed., *Choral-Buch zu den in der Provinz Brandenburg gebräuchlichen Gesangbüchern, Op. 36* (Erfurt, Germany: Gottfhilf Wilhelm Körners Verlag, 1859): hymn 95, available at Deutsche Digitale Bibliothek, https://www.deutsche-digitale-bibliothek.de/ item/4Q26MAUSNBCX7AUSFPPVBALYX2C52XXG (accessed January 18, 2022).

the Wendish avoids the F#. The Ritter version also employs longer values, such as the dotted half note, and abjures the numerous passing notes preferred by the Wends. (In Serbin, passing tones were called the "Wendish slur" and were utilized profusely.[60]) Compare both of these to the version by Johann Sebastian Bach in his *371 Chorales*:

Figure 2.13 J. S. Bach, "Ein feste Burg." (Source: Johann Sebastian Bach, *Vierstimmige Choralgesänge, Erster Theil*, ed. C. P. E. Bach and Johann Philipp Kirnberger [Leipzig: Johann Gottlob Immanuel Breitkopf, 1784]: 12.)

Bach's version is similar to the Wendish melody in that it employs passing tones in the cantus firmus. Of these three tunes, the Wendish is the least complex, from the note values employed to the simpler harmonic arrangement. The Bach version is more artful in the voice leading of the inner voices.

Favoring the isometric versions of the chorales aligned the Wends against some of the other German groups and

---

60 St. Paul, Serbin, organist emeritus Jack Wiederhold remembers these passing tones as always called the "Wendish slur." Wiederhold, personal correspondence with the author, May 26, 2020.

practically all of the nascent LCMS, for whom attachment to the rhythmic chorale represented a signet of orthodoxy. C. F. W. Walther called his St. Louis congregation together for dedicated *Singstunde* in which they would learn the "new" rhythmic versions of the old chorales as found in the aforementioned *Kirchengesangbuch* of the LCMS.[61] Lacking an immediate *Choralbuch* for the LCMS hymnal, Frederick Layritz's *Kern des deutschen Kirchengesangs* (1844) initially served to provide rhythmic chorale accompaniments for two hundred hymns.[62] Describing the situation in the LCMS, an article in the August 1847 issue of *Der Lutheraner*, an editorial from "F. W.," promotes the importance of the rhythmic chorale to Lutheran confessional identity:

> Only a quick glance at the choral literature of the 16th and 17th centuries teach that earlier melodies in the church were completely different than those today. These days no distinction is observed in view of slower versus faster tempos. In the past a distinction was strictly made and hymns were sung in faster tempos that declared joy, and those that expressed pain and sorrow were done more slowly. In times past people would be satisfied with simple, full valued notes and would, as much as possible, avoid passing notes, superfluous embellishments and flourishes . . . At one time spiritual songs moved along resolutely in whole-, half-, quarter- and eighth notes and not only had a regular beat, but also often had syncopation so that, thus, a variation in the meter (the time signature) occurred so the beat never would be quite the same as the worldly beat. Now with respect to time signatures, they all merge into the

---

61 Carl Schalk, *God Song in a New Land* (St. Louis, MO: CPH, 1995): 131.

62 Robin Leaver, "The Chorale: Transcending Time and Culture," *Concordia Theological Quarterly*, Vol. 56, Nos. 2–3 (April–July 1992): 123–44. See also the primary source, Friedrich Layritz's *Kern des deutschen Kirchengesangs: Eine Sammlung von CC. Chorälen meist aus dem 16. und 17. Jahrhundert in ihren ursprünglichen Tönen und Rhythmen mit alterthümlicher Harmonie vierstimmig zum Gebrauche für Kirche und Haus* (Nördlingen, Germany: C. H. Beck, 1844).

same thing, and one note is held for the same length as others so it turns into nothing but a flurry of passing notes on the strong beat. There can be no doubt that the earlier manner of singing was better.[63]

Kilian needed this *Choralbuch* to represent a distinct Wendish identity, which the LCMS itself could neither supply nor support. Yet even his own community was not of one mind; an increasing German population around Serbin and looming German and Wendish intermarriages had magnified the latent problems between the national identities. Consequently, distinct Wendish and German divine services, although a seemingly obvious solution, failed to relieve the pressure from much of the cultural conflict, of which the manner of chorale singing was simply one manifestation.[64]

The keys chosen for the Serbin *Choralbuch* are uniformly high. "Ein feste Burg" is set in E, as opposed to Bach's D or Ritter's C, the latter having settled into common usage. "Allein Gott" is in A instead of F or G, as it was in most *Choralbücher*. In fact, there is a strange preponderance of hymns in A-major, unusual for hymnals then or now, as flat keys were generally preferred because they were seemingly easier to play. Kilian himself makes frequent references to the importance of the organist to have facility in every key. He writes in 1869 of having "worked through the 24 keys of music." He writes of Leubner's training, "I [Kilian] play the hymn melodies without notes

63 "Ein Wort über Kirchenmelodien," *Der Lutheraner*, Vol. 3, No. 25 (August 10, 1847): 139, trans. Joel R. Baseley in *C. F. W. Walther's Original Der Lutheraner*, Vols. 1–3 (Dearborn, MI: Mark V Publications, 2012). Could "F. W." have been Ferdinand Walther?

64 Gotthilf Birkmann, "March 23, 1932—in Memory of Former Pastor Hermann T. Kilian, in Serbin, Texas," *Giddings Deutsches Volksblatt* (March 23, 1932), reconstructed and trans. Ray Martens at https://wendishresearch.org/history-and-culture/people/rev-gotthilf-birkmann/march-23-1932-in-memory-of-former-pastor-hermann-t-kilian-in-serbin-texas/ (accessed July 29, 2020).

in each chosen key." That he would need facility in all the keys suggests that he made the key selection based on practical factors rather than on the precedent of any existing *Choralbuch*. The lack of written scores probably resulted in settling on keys by trial and error, an advantage to Teinert, who apparently had little interest in reading notes or learning new music but could play well by ear what he knew. One can also sympathize with Leubner, who had been thrust into a situation in which he was required not only to learn new versions of the hymns but also to learn them in unusual keys. There may be another consideration. Harmoniums in the nineteenth century, the kind Serbin used for the church's first half century, were tuned to no standard pitch. Modern instruments are generally tuned to A = 440, allowing for consistency and ensemble playing with other instruments. Before that standard developed in the twentieth century, an A on a keyboard could commonly sound anywhere from a G to a B, and sometimes even further afield. At least one Trasyer harmonium heard by this writer sounds a whole step lower than written. This would explain the preponderance of the number of chorales in A-major (as concert G is a common key to sing) and would bring "Ein feste Burg" down to D, which, while still high by modern terms, is consistent with Bach's version. Yet Kilian's small harmonium currently at the Serbin museum is tuned almost perfectly to A = 440. That instrument, however, would have been replaced by the larger Trayser pedal organ that arrived in December 1869, which is no longer extant but on which the *Choralbuch* would have been worked out.[65] Perhaps the tuning of the instrument in the church determined the key of each hymn? Of course, another simple explanation would be that Kilian had a fine tenor voice and simply gravitated to those higher keys.

---

65 Sound samples and introduction to Kilian's first organ courtesy of Jack and Marian Wiederhold of the Wendish Heritage Museum.

There is an additional smattering of annotative ephemera that lends insight into some of these hymns. The scribe explains that the tune for Lied 43, "Ihr Auserwählten Freuet Euch," is a "Lied des Böhmisch Brüder" (literally, the "Bohemian Brethren," sometimes called Moravians), while Lied 56 is a "Lied von Benjamin Schmolck." (Schmolck was a writer of the Bohemian Brethren.) Lied 81 is described as a "Wendische Volkslied," a folk song, as are four other Lieder, while Lied 128, one of three versions of "Warum Soll ich mich den Grämen," another of which is tantalizingly called a "Serbiner Melodie." Is this a tune from Kilian's pen? This melody is listed three consecutive times, with only one reference to one text in the *WG*. Why were other texts of the same meter not listed with any of these three? This would seem to be reasonable and helpful information to provide—unless the hymnic repertoire in Serbin was really limited to a certain number of texts. Another such "Volke Melodie" is found at Lied 197, "Endlich Muss es doch mit der Noth ein Ende Nehmen."

References

Most of the tune entries in the *Choralbuch* display a superscript reference to that particular melody as it corresponds to a hymn number in other *Gesangbücher*. These are not the musical *sources* as explored previously, as the referenced hymnals featured text-only hymns. Additionally and presumably, but not assuredly, these references would only point to hymnals that would have been in use in Serbin. In fact, these references are the most mysterious aspect of this volume, presenting the most questions that cannot be answered with complete assurance. Of the 240 hymns, most have reference numbers to the *WG*, the Sorbian-language hymnal explored in the previous section. However, some hymns have as many as three references to other *Gesangbücher*, and a few have none. The first enigma of these superscriptions is who wrote them and when. They appear not to have been included in the original draft and may have been written later. Unlike the easily legible titles for each hymn entry, the hymnal references are written in smaller *Kurrentschrift*, that antiquated script used in German-speaking lands almost universally before the twentieth century, and not all are decipherable. There are six identifiable hymnals referenced throughout the *Choralbuch*; although it is quite sensible that each hymn would reference the *WG*, the other hymnals are all German, four of the five being from Upper Lusatian lands, but one coming from Cologne on the Rhine. The St. Louis *Kirchengesangbuch* is not referenced at all. Even though it had a presence in Serbin according to Kilian, his *Choralbuch* made no pretense of applicability to the German singing style, which used the *Kirchengesangbuch* of the LCMS. Further mystifying the situation is that these references to other hymnals (except for the *WG*) are quite minimal, one only appearing once, another half a dozen times, a couple others a dozen times. The references are much more numerous at the beginning of the volume but drop off at the end, suggesting that this process was never completed. Most of the hymn tunes in the *Choralbuch* had additional but unnoted corresponding hymn texts in all of the referenced hymnals—missing references to perhaps as many as two hundred hymns in the case of some hymnals, again suggesting that this lack of thoroughness is merely a result of an unfinished process.

An examination of these hymnals indicated by the *Choralbuch* is fraught with difficulties, since it is impossible to ascertain with complete assurance how exactly these references were used. It seems unlikely that they were random *Gesangbücher* floating around the scribe's desk in Addison. They must have had some connection to Serbin, as the *Choralbuch*'s title indicates. It would be sensible if these references, when completed, would have served as references to the hymnals in use by the various subcongregations in Serbin, as these were the days in which hymnals were personal devotional property, carried to church, rather than simply representing fixtures in the pews. (And the reality is that the Serbin Lutherans were divided in manifold ways—by language, by culture, by preference for Saxon liturgy, by preference for conventicles, or by allegiance to particular personalities.) Hymn boards would be useless, and in the days before printed services, perhaps these references were used by the cantor to call out the hymn number in each of the hymnals. Although this can only be posited, the fact that these hymnals are included in the *Choralbuch* indicates some kind of importance to the Serbin community.

Beyond the *WG*, the first hymnal referenced is "Stimmen aus Zion," or more properly, *Stimmen aus Zion oder erbauliche Lieder, zur Verherzlichung Gottes und Erbauung vieler Seelen*, a two-volume hymnal first published in 1744 in Stargard, situated in Pomerania, about 220 miles north of Bautzen. This hymnal, the "Voices from Zion," states in its preface that it is "arranged after the manner of the Porst Gesangbuch." The Porst Gesangbuch can therefore help interpret *Stimmen aus Zion*. Johann Porst (1668–1728), a disciple of Spener and provost of Berlin,[66] published three successive versions of his hymnal, beginning in 1708, all "breathing the Pietism of Spener and the earlier Halle school."[67] In the preface to the 1727 edition, Porst writes that his hymnal is inspired by the "pure milk" of Spener's theology as found in the Order of Salvation.[68] Indeed, both the Porst hymnal and *Stimmen aus Zion* bear many uncanny correlations in the arrangement of their sections. Kilian praises Porst's theological writings in a report of 1840 in Kotitz: "As for the religious instruction in the school, the good religion book of the sainted Porst, Provost and Consistory Council in Berlin

---

66 Samuel Macauley Jackson, ed., *The New Schaff-Herzog Encyclopedia of Religious Knowledge* (New York: Funk & Wagnall's, 1911): 134.

67 Ibid.

68 Johann Porst, *Geistliche und Liebliche Lieder* (Berlin, 1807): introduction.

is still the basic one in use."[69] With such words of approbation, how would Kilian not sanction the use of this related hymnal's contents in his parish?

Another hymnal to which the *Choralbuch* refers is simply called the "Alte Breslauer Gesangbuch," which turns out to be the *Allgemeines und vollständiges Gesangbuch für die Königl. Preuß. Schlesis. Lände*, edited by Johann Friedrich Burg, published in various iterations in the eighteenth century in Breslau, Silesia, now in Poland, but historically a part of Prussia since 1742. Burg (1689–1766), a student (and son-in-law) of Caspar Neumann, the hymn writer, was born and died at Breslau and intended to create a "general and complete Silesian hymnal, the opportunity for which was provided by the reinstitution of public worship in 1742."[70] Unlike Porst, in Burg's long preface, he makes no mention of Spener.

There are six references to the "Freylinghausen Gesangbuch," or "Hallesches Gesangbuch," both colloquial names for the *Geistreiches Gesang-Buch, den Kern alter und neuer Lieder*, compiled by Johann Anastasius Freylinghausen (1670–1739) and first published in 1704; subsequent editions were often called simply the "Halle Gesangbuch" in recognition of Freylinghausen's long association with that city, first as August Hermann Francke's assistant at St. Ulrich's Church, and later as the director of the orphanage. The volume contains 683 texts and 173 melodies, the only book explored here that exhibits some corresponding musical notation. The Freylinghausen hymnal set the standard for eighteenth-century Pietist Gesangbücher, combining as it did the *Kernlieder* of the Reformation with the newer hymns that exude the warmth of Pietism, including 44 of his own. John Julian evaluates this important theologian

69 Kilian, "Kotitz."

70 Johann Friedrich Burg, *Allgemeines und vollständiges Gesangbuch für die Königl. Preuß. Schlesis. Lände* (Breslau, Germany: Johann Jacob Korns, 1751): introduction.

thus: "As a hymnwriter Freylinghausen ranks not only as the best of the Pietistic school, but as the first among his contemporaries. His finest productions are distinguished by a sound and robust piety, warmth of feeling depth of Christian experience, scripturalness, clearness and variety of style, which gained for them wide acceptance."[71] It would have been extraordinary if at least some of the German pilgrims to Serbin did not bring this book with them, so important was this hymnal to Lutheran piety of the day.

There is only one reference to an "Alte Dresdener Gesangbuch," which is certainly *Das Privilegierte Ordentliche und Vermehrte Dreßdnische Gesang-Buch*, published in 1725 in Dresden and Leipzig and reprinted numerous times throughout the eighteenth century.[72] Like the "Alte" applied to the "Breslau Gesangbuch," the writer thought it important to clarify which hymnal was intended here, as the Dresdner hymnals had an important history in the LCMS. The early Saxon immigrants to Missouri had brought the "new" *Dresdnische Gesangbuch* of 1796 with them, using it at Trinity in St. Louis as their primary hymnal. Edited by Karl Christian Tittmann, this volume suffered not from saccharine Pietist hymnody but from an Enlightenment hermeneutic, which probably drove the Missouri Lutherans in 1843 to launch the process for editing a hymnal in which "only pure Lutheran hymns should be used,"[73] ultimately resulting in the *Kirchengesangbuch* of 1847. Walther may have been inspired to create a new hymnal based on the rationalist deficiencies of the "new" Dresden hymnal, so he turned to the "old" Dresden hymnals for inspiration. Jon Vieker notes that "when one examines the older generation

71 John Julian, *A Dictionary of Hymnology* (London: John Murray, 1892): 396.

72 *Das Privilegirte Ordentliche und Vermehrte Dreßdnische Gesang-Buch* (Dresden: Friedrich Hekeln, 1752).

73 "Minutes of Trinity Congregation, St. Louis, Missouri," Concordia Historical Institute, St. Louis, MO, February 3, 1843.

of Dresden hymnals—specifically those published prior to 1796—the outline and organization of the hymns resemble very much the outline that Walther adopted for the hymnal of 1847 . . . for Walther, *KELG* 1847 represented a repudiation of the Rationalist hymnals of his day and a restoration of the 'old,' pre-1796 Dresden line of hymnals."[74] A writer in *Der Lutheraner* in 1850 argues for the importance of relying on these "old" hymnals: "Only the old hymn books—which are also now and then in this land found among immigrant German Lutherans, such as the old Dresden, the old Marburg, the old Silesian, the Pomeranian, Prussian, Hamburger, Bavarian, etc.—exhibit a sufficiently large stock of the old pure Lord's Supper hymns containing the teachings of the Lutheran Church. And whoever has no such old hymnal in his possession, this alone should be enough to convince him to get the 'St. Louis Lutheran Hymnal.'"[75] Here Jan Kilian and C. F. W. Walther were in complete accord, as Kilian's final post in the state church of Saxony had allowed him to encounter and confront the consequences of unrestrained rationalist ideas among the clergy and laity. That many of his congregation should possess "Alte" versions of their respective regional hymnals should have pleased him. There is only one reference to the "Alte Dresdener Gesangbuch" in the *Choralbuch*, although a great majority of the hymn tunes have textual equivalents in that *Gesangbuch*. Perhaps the writer of these superscripts did not own a *Dresdnische Gesangbuch* for reference?

The final hymnal to which the *Choralbuch* refers is a *Coelner Liederschatz*, which so far has not been identified, as this too was not as much a proper name as a colloquial one. The

---

74 Jon Vieker, "Historical Introduction," in *Walther's Hymnal: Church Hymnbook for Evangelical Lutheran Congregations of the Unaltered Augsburg Confession Containing the Most Popular Hymns of the Blessed Dr. Martin Luther and Other Spiritual Teachers*, trans. Matthew Carver (St. Louis, MO: CPH, 2012): xii.

75 Ibid.

reference occurs seven times in the *Choralbuch*. Cologne would have been part of Prussia after 1815, but it was some four hundred miles from the Wendish heartland. A *Liederschatz* is also not synonymous with a hymnal. *Liederschätzen* typically contained more folk songs and could diverge from hymnody that was strictly liturgical or even sacred. They were literally a "treasury" of songs collected often to represent a culture's sacred and secular music.[76] This outlier hymnal, having no regional connection or even spiritual principles that bind the others in common, may evidence that these were representative hymnals of the parish population and that, through an accident of migration, some individuals were using this hymnal in Texas. It must have been a massive volume, as one hymn in the *Choralbuch* refers to *Liederschatz* hymn #1807!

As the first Missouri Synod congregation in Texas, one would expect to find more representation of the *Kirchengesangbuch* of 1847. Yet the *Kirchengesangbuch* would only have been utilized by the German-speaking congregation, who worshipped separately from the Wendish. Kilian's letter from 1869 requesting thirty more such hymnals suggests that there had been some around, presumably within the prior three years, when the congregation joined the synod. Even working under the assumption that the notations in the *Choralbuch* are unfinished, that the *Kirchengesangbuch* did not rank even one entry suggests its lack of relevance to the Wendish community still in 1872.

Arrangement and Explanatory Rubrics

The *WG* provides the underlying method of ordering the *Choralbuch*. Although one might expect the volume to present the melodies alphabetically, as would be most practical, its Lied 1, "Nun freut euch, lieben Christen," corresponds with hymn 1 in the *WG*. The numbers themselves proceed generally

---

76 Carl Schalk, personal correspondence with the author, July 2020.

consecutively, aligning with the hymnal's ordering, with some large swaths in the middle that clearly do not follow the same pattern but return to a semblance of consecutive numbering. This arrangement, although it serves to unify the companion with its parent volume, is a bit impractical for the organist. This again is probably an echo of Kilian's hand, a very practical and logical approach, but not necessarily a configuration an organist would likely employ, as the numbers in the hymnal and the *Choralbuch* would not correspond. A note must be made of the relationship between text and tunes in the *Choralbuch* and the *WG*. The German-language hymn titles in the *Choralbuch* are associated with specific hymn texts, to which they must carefully be applied, unless the *Choralbuch* specifies that a particular tune may apply to more than one text. Of the 240 tunes, there are only 27 instances in which the rubrics indicate that a tune may be used for two or even three texts. In 213 cases, the title of the hymn "tune" also refers to the hymn text, thus allowing for a determination of exactly what hymns were known and sung. Unlike most hymnals of the time, which would provide a tune name under the title, a relatively limited number of hymn tunes supplying the melodies for potentially hundreds of hymns, the *WG*, which is entirely in Wendish, provides a German title translation underneath the Wendish title. Beneath that, the tune name(s) is supplied in Wendish. Some hymns have no German translations, thus lack any German title (there are no instances of this in the *Choralbuch*, however). The hymnal itself also has dual indexes—one for Wendish titles and one for German titles, which ultimately point to the Wendish hymn. The *Choralbuch* lists the hymn titles only in German.

Annotated rubrics provide even more clarity as to performance practices that were particularly unique to the Wends and suggest exactly how different some of their liturgical traditions were, certainly a point of contention between the German and Wendish communities:

- Lied 3, "Du Ewiger Abgrund," is listed as the tune for *WG* 6, 433, and 227. A notation above and a bracket of the second phrase indicate a "variation in Lied 227"—in this case, referring to 227 in the *WG*. The tunes for both Lied 6 ("Du ewiger Abgrund der seligen") and 433 ("Sei Fröhlich im Herren") are associated with the Bohemian Brethren and have a poetic meter of 12.8.12.8.10.10.12.12, with a total of eighty-six syllables, while Lied 227 has a slightly different meter of seventy-three syllables. Presumably, the bracketed section would be omitted if sung to Lied 227.
- Lied 12, "Jehovah ist mein Hirt," Freylinghausen's setting of Psalm 23, bears the rubric, "The last four stanzas are sung in the same manner as the last four stanzas." What this means for this fourteen-stanza hymn is unclear.
- Lied 14, "Gott der Vater Wohn uns bei," demonstrates a particular problem with Wendish hymnody, as the rubric notes, "The Wendish translation of this song has in the first of each stanza an extra syllable." Inconsistent syllables and metrical problems seemed endemic to Wendish hymnody from the earliest centuries, causing much confusion to congregations.[77] A similar explanation is given to Lied 47, "Christ lag in Todesbanden," in which the "Wendish text of this hymn has in the first and third line of each verse two extra syllables," then briefly continues indecipherably. That the German congregation had to live with the Wendish hymnic tradition is made clear in Lied 96, "Komm, Heiliger Geist, Herre Gott," which has the observation, "The bracketed notes are for the German text of the hymn." In this case, this adds another extra note for an extra syllable. This suggests that the *Choralbuch* was used, at least on occasion, to accompany German singing. Was the German congregation, who worshipped at a different time in the same building as the Wendish, forced to sing the awkward Wendish metrical iterations of the German chorales, as this notation implies? The evidence seems to indicate they were, and one can understand the strife this would cause between ethnicities. The Wendish and German communities eventually grew more

---

77 Stone, "Sorbian Hymn."

distinct, with the German congregation utilizing Karl Brauer's *Mehrstimmiges Choralbuch*, with its accompaniments suited for the versions of the chorales presented in the 1847 *Kirchengesangbuch*. This book was not published until 1888, however; until then, the two communities would struggle in their hymn singing.

- Lied 20, "Nun Komm der Heiden Heiland," has an instruction that "in Serbin, one sings this Advent hymn to the following melody," which at that point is illegible. Apparently, Wendish tradition permits extracting an ancient text/tune pairing in favor of a more preferred tune!

- Lied 103, "Durch Adams Fall," notes that "in Serbin, hymn 303 is sung to this melody." A similar rubric is given for Lied 111, "Wir wollen singen heut."

- Both Lieder 131 and 132 are entitled "Mir nach, spricht Christus, unser Held," but the second is noted as being "andere Weise" (another way) to sing the hymn. The fact that two melodies are offered as an option for this hymn suggests that this practice was the exception rather than the rule.

- At least one note is historical: Lied 209, "Jesulein, man kann es Lesen," has an explanatory superscript describing the tune as an "old melody: Quem pastores laudavere," which it is indeed recognizably so.

- Lied 234, "Ach bleib mit deiner Gnade," contains the intriguing observation that it is a folk song with the rubric that after every half verse, one is to sing "Befiehl du Deine Wege."

- Lied 239 is simply titled "The same text, but a newly-entered Würtemb. Melody." Presumably, this refers to the previous Lied, "Es glanzet der Christen," whose text can be replaced with this melody from the Württemberg collection. Does this refer to the *Choralbuch* or to the "Württembergische Gesangbuch"? This volume served as the basic accompaniment edition to the Wollenweber Gesangbuch in use by the local Texas Synod, so there does exist the possibility that Kilian encountered this tune from his Texas Synod brethren.

- Lied 81 is associated with two titles in the *WG*, "O Wie Selig sind die Seelen" and, in parentheses, "Alles ist an

Gottes Segen," with an explanatory rubric that the tune in the *Choralbuch* is a "Wendisch Volkslied" (folk song) and that "in this church, this hymn is sung in the way of 531," presumably meaning that the tune may apply to both texts.

- Lied 103, "Durch Adams Fall," is applied to 141 in the hymnal but notes that "in Serbin, this melody is sung for no. 303," which is the hymn "Was Mein Gott Will." Both have 8.7.8.7 D meters. A similar rubric is applied to Lied 111, "Wir Wollen Sing Heut," which "may be sung to the melody of #77," which is the familiar "Jesu, Meine Freude." Here the rubric is less explicit—instead of stating that a particular chorale will (*wird*) be sung to a particular text, this one seems to allow a choice (*dürfen*). Perhaps one tune would be more familiar to the Germans than to the Wends?

- No title is given to Lied 184, which is simply called "Wendische Volksmelodie," which may be applied to hymns 33 and 384 in the hymnal.

These last few instances obliquely reinforce the Wendish practice of associating most texts with only one tune and specifying very clearly when that is not necessarily the case. Although normally hymn tunes can supply any number of texts as long as the meter corresponds, the titles of the Lieder in the *Choralbuch* refer specifically to that one hymn text—the one that provides the title for the Lied—and are not necessarily interchangeable with other texts of that same meter. As can be seen in some of the previous analyses, it seems these melodies had been compiled very specifically for the Wendish translations, even to the point of carefully noting when the German text would differ or when the melody would have to be amended to correspond with an unusual Wendish translation. This would suggest that the hymn repertoire in Serbin was no more than what is represented in this *Choralbuch*—some 240 hymn texts to supply the entire liturgical year. This is not a negligible number of hymn texts for a congregation to know, even for the modern church, especially when the pastor was attempting to navigate in two languages. Since the *Choralbuch*'s tune names correspond to the actual hymn texts, it is possible to ascertain what exactly the Serbin Wends were singing during these early years. There are a few additional incidental notations, but most are simply aids to reference other Lieder in the volume. About ten individual rubrics cannot be interpreted due to ink degradation or indecipherable script. A couple could be additional references to *Gesangbücher*. The care, concern, and painstaking detail with which the annotator conveyed information in this book suggests someone with great investment in the process, but the handwriting does not match Jan Kilian's. Gerhard certainly was involved in the production of the volume, if for no other reason than he conveyed his father's notes to the scribe in Addison, presumably supervising its production. Yet Gerhard was scarcely twenty years old in 1872, and although according to his father he had received a solid musical education in Addison, he certainly would not have been as cognizant about Wendish liturgical practice as his father had been. Gerhard had been living in Addison since the age of sixteen and had himself played very few times (but at least two) at Serbin. He seems unlikely to have had such detailed knowledge of Wendish hymnic practice. That is not to say he could not have added these notations later in life.

These details, then, constitute very specifically what Kilian had attempted to teach the recalcitrant Teacher Leubner as to the "Wendish way" of singing. And certainly, there must have been other peculiarities that went unwritten and that have been lost to history. One can sympathize with Leubner's frustration in having to learn an unfamiliar way of leading congregational singing, and one can also discern how the application of such musical details would only divide the Wends and the Germans in Serbin. Each was acquainted with their own way, neither group accustomed to accommodating the other, and each eschewing any sort of change, as Kilian suggests in at least one letter. Although one hesitates to arrive at the conclusion, it may fairly be said that sacred music in Serbin served more to divide than to unify. Music certainly was not the only factor, and likely only proceeded from ingrained cultural animosities. If it is true, however, that sacred music provides an indispensable vehicle for prayer, praise, and proclamation within the liturgy, it is not surprising that these Wendish Lutherans held their views with passionate potency.

3

Kilian as Composer, Hymn Writer, and Liturgist

Tangential to an analysis of Wendish Lutheran music in Texas has been Jan Kilian's own background as a composer and hymn writer, vocations that were largely eclipsed by his leading a migration to Texas. Yet as the founder and first representative of the LCMS in Texas, his creative background deserves some review.

Jan Kilian had some musical training in Europe, often composing melodies for his poems. His tunes are in the character of the late Romantic era, but he was skilled enough to compose in different styles. His melody to "Journey through the Sea of Life," written to accompany his poem in the astoundingly particular meter of 11.9.11.9.11.9.11.9, is reminiscent of a folk song, and roughly in Bar, or AAB, form, with the first two melodic lines (called *Stollen*) exactly the same, concluding with a contrasting B section (called *Abgesang*) and a brief coda.[1] Such was the folk style that Luther and many of the early Reformation hymnists employed in many of their chorales, including "A Mighty Fortress." The text exemplifies what Kilian hoped Wendish folk singing would be—a secular narrative, perhaps,

---

1 Zersen, *Poetry and Music*: 26. Rev. Martin Doering is responsible for the hymn translations in this book.

but undergirded with God's Word and promises. Written in 1851, this hymn anticipates the great migration of the Wends.[2]

Figure 3.1 "Through the Wind-Driven Waves" from Kilian's *Spěwarske wjesele* (*Joyful Singing*). (Source: David Zersen, ed., *The Poetry and Music of Jan Kilian* [Austin: Concordia University Press, 2010]: 26. Courtesy of David Zersen and Martin Doering, translator.)

In a similar lyric style is his "Awakening to Song," also to the complex metrical scheme of 8.7.8.7.8.8.6.6, its range of just more than an octave quite consistent with folk music, and similarly set in Bar form, the joyous F-major key a suitable expression of his text: "O, praise the Lord with joyful songs!"[3] These two songs might be considered more in the folk realm, in both text and tune. But Kilian also honed his craft in composing melodies with a more ecclesiastical air. His "You Are Members of Christ's Body" has the hallmark of many of his preferred

2 Ibid.

3 Ibid.: 20.

melodies in the *Choralbuch*. The rhythm is simple, reminiscent of the isorhythmic chorales the Wends preferred. The melody constitutes a succession of quarter notes moving stepwise, punctuated by three instances of eighth note passing tones, and its subject matter is scriptural.[4]

Figure 3.2 "You are Members of Christ's Body" from Kilian's *Spěwarske wjesele (Joyful Singing)*. (Source: Zersen, *Poetry and Music*: 54. Courtesy of David Zersen and Martin Doering, translator.)

His 1846 hymn "Happiness in Hope," set in the simple meter of 9.9.9.8 and of only two lines, no doubt sought to reassure the Wends in their journey: "There is a brightness in God's city, an invitation, seen from afar. The wasteland's wand'ring soon is over; we're moving to our guiding star."[5] He seemed to have composed two tunes for this text, an earlier version having been arranged for soprano, alto, tenor, and bass (SATB) by Bjarnat Krawc in 1926.

Krawc (1861–1948), also known as Bernhard Schneider, a Sorbian composer, choir director, and teacher, arranged a number of Kilian's melodies for four-part SATB in 1926. Krawc studied in Bautzen and Dresden, where in 1918 he was appointed as the Saxon court music director. In 1926, he founded the first Sorbian-language musical journal, and shortly thereafter,

---

4 Ibid.: 54.
5 Ibid.: 30.

Figure 3.3 "Through the Wind-Driven Waves" as originally printed in the music edition to Kilian's *Spěwarske wjesele* (*Joyful Singing*), published in 1847. (Source: Provided by the author.)

a Sorbian orchestra. Having composed chamber music, piano pieces, and orchestral works, his interest also lay in sacred and traditional Wendish music, having even composed *Wendische Volkslieder für eine Singstimme und Klavier*, op. 52.[6] His interest in traditional Wendish music turned his attention to Kilian's songs, and he arranged at least six of Kilian's melodies for SATB. Now in the Sorbisches Kulturarchiv in Bautzen, these manuscript scores date from 1926 to 1939 and are settings of Kilian melodies from 1846, 1847, and 1849, all certainly from *Spěwarske wjesele* (*Joyful Singing*), of which versions after 1846 introduced Kilian's tunes.

---

6 For a more thorough review of Schneider and the Sorbian nationalist school, see Teresa Nowak and Tomasz Nowak, "The Work of Sorbian Composers and the Issue of Their National Identity," *Musicology Today* (December 2011): 192–204.

Figure 3.4 Sorbian composer Bjarnat Krawc arranged some of Kilian's melodies for SATB. (Source: https://upload.wikimedia.org/wikipedia/commons/9/92/Bjarnat_Krawc.jpg.)

The Serbin *Choralbuch* concludes with an *Anhang* containing a four-part setting of Psalm 23 composed by Kilian and carefully rendered by Gerstenberger. Unlike his hymns and songs, for which he only composed a melody line, this is a harmonized melody of thirty-eight measures, with no attribution of the harmonization to anyone else. Did he compose this motet in Texas, or was it recycled from earlier in his life? Perhaps this musical endeavor resulted from Kilian's years of musical study in Texas as he attempted to teach Leubner; perhaps Kilian felt more confident twenty-five years after his initial forays into musical composition.

Jan Kilian's early literary efforts had dealt in translations, including in 1838 of a short book of Samuel Lucius, "containing information for all who wished to be faithful Lutherans."[7] In 1841 and 1842, he rendered into Wendish certain works of Johann Phillip Fresenius (1705–61), a moderate Lutheran theologian who had been influenced by Spener. Forthwith, Kilian turned his efforts to Pietist theologian Johann Porst and to the

---

7 Nielsen, *Johann Kilian*: 13.

Figure 3.5 Kilian's motet setting of Psalm 23 from his *Choralbuch*. (Source: Jan Kilian, ed., *Choralbuch für evangel. luth. Gemeinde in Serbin, Texas* [n.p., 1872].)

Silesian hymn writer Karl Heinrich von Bogatzky (1690–1774);
Kilian rendered Bogatzky's beloved *Güldenes Schatz-Kästlein der
Kinder Gottes* into Wendish.[8] Kilian's *Spěwarske wjesele* (*Joyful
Singing*) in 1846 represented his first foray into poetic writing. It is
a short booklet of twenty-eight songs, both his own and his translations; he would eventually compose music for them in a subsequent edition. Later in the 1840s, he would translate and publish
the Lutheran confessional books. Ultimately, Kilian would write
some one hundred hymns that would end up in Wendish hymnals, both Lutheran and Reformed, to the present day.

Kilian saw himself as a member of the Wendish literary and
social intelligentsia, although his concern for uniting the
Wendish language with the Lutheran faith would isolate him
philosophically from his peers, and he was largely left "alone
among his contemporaries, isolated and unique,"[9] although he
has been called "a religious hero" who "surpass[es] all of our
hymn writers."[10] His hymn "Wěrjacebo skóržba" ("A Believer's
Desire"), written early in his career to lament his isolation from
the Wendish literati, could prophetically apply to his situation
after arriving in Texas:

> *Oh, I dearly would my Jesus see!*
> *I would join the angel throng!*
> *God's creation all is beautiful,*
> *but my worries fill my songs.*

> *Here I wander over lonesome roads;*
> *No companions walk with me—*
> *Bitter sorrow, never tasting joy,*
> *Alien to all I see.*

---

8 Carl Heinrich von Bogatzky, Gottried Leske, and Jan Kilian, *Khorlje Hain-
   richa Bogatzkeho słoty Schaz-Kaschczik bożich Dżjeczi* (W Budyschini:
   Reichel, 1847).

9 Rudolf Jentsch, *Stawizny serbskebo pismowstwa* (Bautzen: Domowina,
   1954), quoted in Malinkowa, introduction: 10.

10 Jentsch, quoted in ibid.

My supporters have abandoned me;
Now they wait for my demise,
Searching, waiting for a fault in me:
Some misstep, some furtive ties.

In their anger others scowl at me
While I walk in the pilgrim way.
Since my Savior Christ is by my side,
Foes torment me every day.

Scoffers make their ugly jokes on me;
They despise my feeble light.
Souls ungrateful—never thankful praise—
They deny the Father's right.

This derision pains my spirit so:
My Lord Jesus is blasphemed.
Every person seeks his prize below:
Called to bear a cross? A dream!

"God's elect shall live by faith alone,"
Yet I struggle mightily.
Spirit, help me put that armor on
That will save and strengthen me.

Once in heaven I shall find rest
That my weary soul desires.
I am yearning for that blessed peace,
For the end of sorrow's fires.

Marantha! Jesus, quickly come;
Let me wear the robes so bright.
All creation shall find unity;
No more sorrow; no more night.[11]

---

11 Zersen, *Poetry and Music*: 18–19. Permission to reproduce granted by David Zersen and Martin Doering.

This first-person, subjective hymn recalls Psalm 137, a dirge for hopeless times of "captivity," either literal or figurative, a recurring theme in Kilian's life. These words indeed sound as if they could have been written at any point during Kilian's later career in Texas rather than in 1846.

Jan Kilian, always considered the stalwart of orthodoxy he certainly was, could be motivated occasionally by latent Pietistic tendencies that could have been appropriated from the Zeitgeist, as from the more tangible influences, such as the semi-Pietist volumes he translated in the 1830s and 1840s. His hymnody, while grounded in Scripture and firmly within the pale of Lutheran orthodoxy, bears hallmarks of the Pietist tradition he knew so well and of which he was most certainly an heir. One hymn "popularly sung in German in Serbin" exhibits some of these tendencies:

> Transforming will of love, fulfill your plan in me;
> Your kingdom, my desire; with You my peace shall be.
> From You I have the Word; Salvation now is heard.
>
> Eternal, living Word, take root and grow in me;
> Enlighten me, that I may serve you fruitfully.
> Direct me with your might; and lead me through the night.
>
> O strong and faithful hand, protect and fashion me;
> Erase my errors, Lord; Cleanse all impurities.
> Give me the garments fair That I your Feast may share.[12]

This hymn is an intensely introspective prayer for personal transformation, exhorting God to "transform," "enlighten," "protect," "fashion," and "cleanse" so that one may "grow" in order that this faith may enable one to "serve [God] faithfully." Here Kilian connects faith and life, although the awareness of Word and Sacrament in this process is confirmed. Kilian usually

---

12 Ibid.: 52.

manages some reference to the world's fleeting ephemera, contrasting the security of God's presence with the inconstancy of the world; here he prays to "lead me through the night." Whether in Europe or in Texas, Kilian seemed always ready to depart this world for the next. In a rather tender and emotive poem written "At the Grave of a Dear Son," Kilian bewails the death of eleven-month-old Nathanael Martin Kilian with a palatable sense of his own expectation for the eschaton:

> *Therefore I wish you a good night, my dear.*
> *Oh I wish I would sleep soon too,*
> *As you sleep here after a short suffering!*
> *The whole world I would refuse*
> *To join you in the house of God*
> *And to receive you forever;*
> *Have a good night.*[13]

Kilian's early formative experiences, both personal and otherwise, certainly colored his leadership and decisions after his arrival in Texas.

A careful analysis of the Serbin *Choralbuch* also allows a glimpse into Kilian's own theological constructs and proclivities, even discounting for a moment any musical implications. Returning to this volume, each Lied—a tune associated in most cases with one particular hymn text, unless noted otherwise—represents a hymn sung in Serbin selected by the parish pastor, the selection of hymns just as important then as today. Thus, determining the types of hymns and hymn writers Kilian preferred can elucidate somewhat on Kilian's complicated and nuanced mind. Of the 240 chorales in the book, four are alternate melodies for a given text, leaving 236 chorales remaining. Eight chorale entries are double-titled with two hymn texts. These additional four alternate texts increase the number of hymn texts back to 240. There are some hymns for

---

13 Ibid.: 49.

whom an author could not be ascertained, but of those that can be determined, the following observations emerge:

- Thirty-one hymns, or 13 percent of the *Choralbuch* contents, are Martin Luther's hymns, whether originals or translations. This does not include a smattering of other Reformation-era hymns by Elisabeth Cruciger, Nicolai, Georg Rhau and the *Klug Gesangbuch*, Kaspar Fuger, Nicolaus Hermann, Nicolaus Decius, Ludwig Helmbold, and a few others who represent the sixteenth century. Luther's work is well represented. For comparison, C. F. W. Walther's *Kirchengesangbuch* of 1847, out of 443 total hymns, contained 38 by Luther, or about 9 percent.
- Kilian leaned heavily on Silesians, of which at least ten hymn writers of any era can be considered Silesian by some definition. This includes 11 hymns by Michael Weiße (ca. 1488–1534), a contemporary of Luther who had joined the Bohemian Brethren and whose hymnal of 1531 provided some of the *Kernlieder* of the Reformation. By contrast, Walther's 1847 hymnal would include only 6 hymns by Weiße. Nine other hymn writers represented the Silesian tradition in the *Choralbuch*: M. von Löwenstern (3), Johann Heermann (3), Benjamin Schmolck (3), Angelus Silesius (2), Martin Behm (2), Christian Knorr (1), Aegidius Rother (1), Johan Andreas Roth (1), Johannes Gigas (1), and Christopher Tietze (1).
- Kilian included 11 hymns by Paul Gerhardt.
- The Pietist writers, either Lutheran or Reformed, arguably provided most of the substance of the *Choralbuch*. Some of the more identifiable, in addition to many of those Silesians mentioned previously, include Christian Richter, Gottfried Arnold, Johann Herrnschmidt, Johann Joseph Winkley, Johann Schroeder, Johann Rist, Joachim Neander, Bartolomäus Crasselius, Christian Bernstein, Johann Lehr, Simon Dach, Adam Drese, Johann Freystein, Ernst Buchfelder, Johann Friedrich Hertzog, and Leopold Lehr. Ten of these hymns come directly from the "Freylinghausen Gesangbuch," a book representing the great Halle Pietist tradition. In contrast, Walther's contemporary

Kirchengesangbuch of the LCMS included 1 hymn from Arnold and none of Richter's.

- The Bohemian Brethren, otherwise known as the Unitas Fratrem or simply the "Moravians," find generous representation in the *Choralbuch*. Applied categories here quite unhelpfully overlap. Michael Weiße, an early clergyman in the Unitas Fratrem, has as many hymns as the Lutheran writer Gerhardt and stands second only to Luther himself in representation. Bohemian Brethren hymns generally possess that introspective air of Pietism, so they can overlap with that category. The Wends' close proximity to the Bohemian Brethren probably facilitated an interchange of hymns. According to Gerald Stone, "Sorbian religious life in the eighteenth century was influenced by the settlement of Moravian Brethren at Herrnhut, established in 1772 on land donated by the Sorbophil and Pietist, Nikolaus Ludwig, Graf von Zinzendorf (1700–60). Herrnhut is only about six miles outside traditional Sorbian territory, to the south-east of Lubij (Löbau). Von Zinzendorf is the author of about 2,000 hymns, fourteen of which, in Sorbian translation, found their way into the Sorbian Lutheran hymnal."[14]

Indeed, Zinzendorf himself is represented by three hymns in the *Choralbuch*, one for which (Lied 3) he provided both a text and a tune. The annotator of the *Choralbuch* even writes a note on Lied 23, observing that it is a "Lied des Böhmische Brüder" (hymn of the Bohemian Brethren). The source for Lied 209 is ascribed to the hymnal for the "Gesangbuch der Brüdergemeinder" (congregation of the brethren). Lied 43 also comes from the Bohemian Brethren. Although Bohemian, if not Unitas Fratrem, the reformer Jan Hus is represented by "Jesus Christ, Unser Heiland," which Walther also included in his hymnal.

Having been uprooted and leaving their homes due to theological upheavals, Kilian certainly realized that the Wends must remain rooted in their faith and in their traditions in order to

---

14 Stone, "Sorbian Hymn": 88.

survive as Lutherans in the harsh environment of Texas. Kil-ian's own hymns contributed to creating a shared culture of these Texas Lutherans according to one account of Wendish singing from 1883:

> Finally they sing the common Sorbian church hymns from "Hymns of Joy" that Kilian had published in Bautzen in 1858 [*sic*]. Most frequently and most dearest are the songs they sing: "The Heavens are Bedecked with Clouds," "The Good Gifts on Earth," "Come Heart and Rejoice," "May All Act Thereon," "Give Praise You Lovely Blossoms," and that one with the lovely melody "Our Ship Sails the Sea." And when these songs have died away, then a very special one is struck up, namely: "When Again We See Each Other," and the old eyes weep; the young fold their hands: God's Peace—encompassing peace, that is the song with which they once said "Farewell" to their brothers and sisters at home—forever.[15]

If there was ever a time for spiritual innovation, which was so against the nature of his people anyway, it would not be during a time of upheaval. Kilian and his congregation needed the familiar. The Texas Lutherans were a good fifteen years behind the Missouri Lutherans, who had established their own Zion on the Mississippi and had the resources to publish and com-municate, to interact with others, to learn rhythmic chorales, to catechize properly, and just generally to reclaim the cause of orthodoxy. These were luxuries Kilian recognized he did not possess, and he was sorrowful for it.

Of Jan Kilian's many contributions to Texan, Wendish, and Lutheran culture, his "Agenda" could have been one of the most important, except that an accident of history had tucked it out of the public gaze for many years. Through the 1980s and 1990s, Texan writer Daphne Garrett researched the *Deutsches*

---

15 "Kosyk to editor, [Luzica] [Translated from summary to Dr. Cyz]," Texas Wends: Letters and Documents, https://forum.wendishresearch.org/viewthread.php?tid=3368 (accessed January 20, 2022).

Volksblatt, the Wendish-language newspaper serving Central Texas from 1899 to 1949 and published in Giddings, Texas, only a few miles from Serbin. Her investigations took her to the home of the daughter of the original owner of the paper,[16] where Garrett uncovered in Hattie Proske Hilsberg's home in Giddings a number of printed but unbound copies of Kilian's "Agenda," a supplementary liturgical volume intended for use at Serbin. Kilian compiled the "Agenda" for publication in 1883, likely for the use of his son Hermann, who that same year would graduate from seminary to accept the call to Serbin, relieving his father. Jan Kilian died the next year, the congregation never having used the liturgy. It would remain concealed until, inexplicably, it was printed in 1909 by J. A. Proske, who also published the *Deutsches Volksblatt*. Yet the "Agenda" was never bound, and several copies remained in Ms. Hilsberg's home until their discovery by Garrett.

The "Agenda" is likely most significant for being the first book to be published in the Sorb language in the United States. Its liturgical origins are enigmatic, as it seems not to be any translation from Walther, but it is likely Kilian's own, or at least inspired by Wendish liturgical volumes. The "Agenda" is not a liturgy but more properly a collection of prayers and antiphons organized according to the liturgical year, perhaps in modern terms more of an "altar book," although it contains no Scripture readings. A particularly unique feature of the Wendish Lutheran liturgy, at least in Serbin, was the inclusion of scriptural antiphons spoken or sung at the beginning of the service in alternation by the pastor and the congregation. At any rate, there are two prayers along with two antiphons for

16 Daphne Garrett, preface to the *Giddings Deutsches Volksblatt (1899–1949): A History of the Newspaper and Print Shop of the Texas Wends* (Warda, TX: Garrett Historical Research, 1998), available at https://wendishresearch.org/historical/people/daphne-garrett/giddings -deutsches-volksblatt-1899-1949-by-daphne-garrett/ (accessed September 15, 2020).

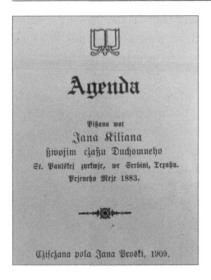

Figure 3.6 Jan Kilian's "Agenda" was published in 1909, but it was never bound and thus received no distribution. (Source: Texas Wendish Heritage Society Museum and Archives, photo taken by the author.)

each Sunday. The congregation would have sung the regular ordinary of the liturgy according to Saxon custom.

A later document in the hand of Hermann Kilian, who had replaced his father as the pastor at Serbin, contains hymn assignments and introductory antiphons for most Sundays of the liturgical year. This demonstrates the importance of that opening antiphon, as it appears every Sunday. At least by that time, the church had established a pattern of singing two hymns apportioned over three points in the morning services. In addition to the usual entrance hymn, the sermon hymn, or "hymn of the day," would be split into two portions, with the last two stanzas usually sung only at the end of the service.[17] Communion services required two extra hymns for distribution.[18]

---

17 "Hermann Kilian's Note for His Organist," n.d., courtesy of Weldon Mersiovsky.

18 Communion would be celebrated rather infrequently relative to modern times. Even into the 1940s, the Serbin congregation celebrated communion only quarterly (Buchhorn, *Collection of Histories*: 83). Holy Cross, Warda, had voted to observe "Wendish communion services" eight times a year in June 1875. Although this does not state whether this

Trudla Malinkowa assesses Kilian's hymnic endeavors, noting his use of "poetic forms from both pious directions [pietism and orthodoxy] to create dignified church hymns for the worship service, general songs of comfort, and above all, songs of meditation and discipleship filled with biblical references."[19] A theologian alone in Texas whose time was occupied with the squabbles and mundane activities of running a parish, Kilian's creative energy would find much less expression in Serbin than it had in Europe, undoubtedly contributing to his increasing sense of frustration later in his career. Exasperated as he was in Texas, considering it toward the end of his life his "punishment . . . that I must continue as the pastor in Serbin," this joy of singing would he nurture and encourage in his sometimes intractable parishioners. He writes in his *Spěwarske wjesele* (*Joyful Singing*) of 1846,

> Where the church of God stands in living strength, there the people are nowhere ashamed to sing spiritual hymns, be it in a city or village, at home or out-of-doors, on the mountains or in valleys, in solitude or in society. But where people are ashamed to sing spiritual hymns, there life is not worth living; there is the end of tranquil joy; there you can hear the sad sound of songs that were learned at godless spinning gatherings and baptismal feasts. This is the sound of the losers! Seductive and destructive is the singing of secular songs, but useful and constructive is the singing of spiritual hymns.[20]

Nonetheless, all his failures, self-perceived or actual, and all his manifold successes were permeated with the idea that sacred singing is integral to the Christian life, and this sense of the importance of singing remained unchanged throughout his life and shaped those first LCMS Christians in Texas.

---

represents an increase or decrease, the course of Eucharistic practice elsewhere suggests this would have been an increase.

19 Zersen, *Poetry and Music*: 11.

20 Ibid.: 10.

4

The First Pipe Organs and Early Musical Practices

The Lutheran Church experienced exponential growth during the second half of the nineteenth century, the LCMS itself claiming sixteen congregations in Texas by 1884[1] and expanding to sixty-four by 1906, the largest being St. Paul, Serbin, with 632 baptized members, followed by its nearby daughter congregation, Holy Cross, Warda, numbering 610 souls.[2] Holy Cross had been formed in 1873 at the prompting of Jan Kilian's former organist, Carl Teinert, and after a brief stint in the Texas Synod, it was formally accepted into the LCMS in 1874.[3] A fine church building with a painted chancel and elevated pulpit, similar to St. Paul in Serbin, was dedicated in 1881, in which "the organ was located in the center and pews for seating were located at each side wall."[4] This melodeon, or small reed organ, had been purchased in 1875 from a Mr. Urban in Giddings.[5] This little organ provided music for the church for eighteen years until Holy Cross purchased its first pipe organ, which also happened to be the first pipe organ in an LCMS church in Texas.

---

1 Koenig, *Pause to Ponder*: 34.
2 Ibid.: 64.
3 *125 Years of God's Grace*: 5.
4 Ibid.: 7.
5 Ibid.: 84.

Figure 4.1 Holy Cross Lutheran Church, Warda, Texas. (Source: Texas Wendish Heritage Society Museum and Archives, photo #0513.)

On June 14, 1891, the voters' assembly had "resolved to buy a tracker pipe organ built by J. G. Pfeffer of St. Louis, Missouri. In 1892, the old organ was given to the newly formed Trinity Lutheran congregation in LaGrange. The new organ was a hand pump [*sic*] pipe organ."[6] Initially, the choice of this distant, Roman Catholic organ builder may seem an incongruous option for this Texas country church. John George Pfeffer was born in 1823 in Germany, arriving in the United States with the great immigration of 1854.[7] He was likely already trained as an organ builder in Germany but by 1859 had moved to St. Louis, where he lists himself as an "organ technician."[8] In 1865,

6 Ibid.: 84.

7 Douglas Bush and Richard Kassell, eds., *The Organ: An Encyclopedia* (Oxford: Taylor & Francis, 2004): 409.

8 Rosalind Mohnsen and Earl L. Miller, organists, *A Pfeffer Odyssey*, LP, liner notes by William Van Pelt from material supplied by Donald T. Petering et al. (Richmond: Organ Historical Society, 1982).

C. F. W. Walther had commissioned him to build a thirty-four-rank organ for Trinity Church in St. Louis,[9] establishing for the builder a reputation in the LCMS of which it would be said that "a St. Louis pastor in the pulpit and a Pfeffer organ in the gallery was the test of sound Lutheranism."[10] No opus list exists for the firm, which was eventually acquired by George Kilgen upon Pfeffer's death in 1910, but the company's output probably numbered between two hundred and six hundred organs, a goodly number of which had been installed in LCMS churches, including two at the Addison Seminary, which further cemented Pfeffer's reputation in the LCMS. Although the organ at Holy Cross is no longer extant, according to Jack Wiederhold, organist emeritus in Serbin who is familiar with the removal of the instrument decades ago, the organ was visually and tonally similar to the circa 1860 instrument at St. Martin's Roman Catholic Church in Starkenburg, Missouri, with a single manual of an 8 Principal, 8 Salicional, 8 Gedeckt (with inverted mouths), 4 Octave, and 2 Octave, with a pedal 16 Subbass of twenty notes.[11] Although this organ represents one of the smaller instruments of the firm's output and was likely a stock model, in general, "Pfeffer organs are a unique American entity, amalgamating Germanic voicing principles with the growing influence of Boston and English organs."[12] Selecting Pfeffer to build its organ situated the Warda congregation within the larger context of national Lutheranism and the Missouri Synod, affirming its orthodoxy and importance within the region's congregations. This particular selection of an organ builder signaled to the greater Missouri Synod community, whether in Texas or beyond, that Holy Cross had

---

9 Jon Vieker, "C. F. W. Walther: Editor of Missouri's First and Only German Hymnbook," *Concordia Historical Institute Quarterly*, Vol. 65, No. 2 (Summer 1992): 57.

10 Mohnsen and Miller, *Pfeffer Odyssey*.

11 Jack Wiederhold indicates that the organ pictured and described at Starkenburg, Missouri, is similar to the organ previously at Warda.

12 Mohnsen and Miller, *Pfeffer Odyssey*.

developed beyond a parochial expression of an immigrant community in the distant Texas countryside to an important outpost of Word and Sacrament.

If the purchase of a pipe organ represents a "liturgical luxury" that only established, healthy churches could afford, then the next couple of decades represented great prosperity in the Texas Lutheran churches. A Kilgen organ installed at Houston's First German Evangelical Lutheran Church (now First Lutheran) in 1903 represents the first pipe organ in any Lutheran church in that area.[13] Although then a member of the Texas Synod, this had been the church of Rev. Caspar Braun, a correspondent with Jan Kilian and sometime-member of the Missouri Synod. Kilian's own church, St. Paul in Serbin, now under the leadership of Jan's son Rev. Hermann Kilian, purchased a pipe organ in 1904 from Ed Pfeifer, a German immigrant who had launched an organ-building enterprise in nearby Austin in 1888. A member of the Texas Synod's St. Martin's Lutheran Church in Austin, Pfeifer built only five organs, of which only two are extant, including the one at St. Paul Lutheran Church in Serbin, an instrument that so exemplifies his style. The single-manual tracker instrument of ten ranks exhibits Victorian facade pipework elaborately and colorfully stenciled, with gentle voicing. This instrument is the oldest organ in its original location serving an LCMS church in Texas.

St. Paul Lutheran Church, Serbin, Texas, Ed Pfeifer (1904)

Manual:

8 Octave Bass	4 Viol d'Amour
8 Prinzipal	4 Octave
8 Dulciana	3 Quint
8 Doppel Flute	2 Wald Flute
8 Viol d'Gamba	

---

13 "Special Announcement," *Houston Post* (June 3, 1902): 7.

Pedal:
16 Subbass

Manual-Pedal Coupler
Bellows signal

In 1905, Pfeifer built his next organ for Zion Lutheran Church (LCMS) in Walburg, a town north of Austin, established in 1888 by Wendish settlers from Serbin who sought to farm the fertile soils of the region.

Even North Texas keenly felt the Wendish influence. A group of German Lutherans had begun worshipping in Dallas in the 1870s, receiving a couple of years of pastoral care from Rev. J. A. Proft. Of Wendish background, Proft had trained as a cabinetmaker in Bautzen and had even assisted in crafting the windows at St. Paul in Serbin before he was appointed pastor at Trinity, Fedor, Texas, a daughter congregation of Serbin.[14] Zion Lutheran Church in Dallas was organized in 1879, largely from the impetus of brothers Ludwig and Carl Axe, who also donated a melodeon to provide for the church's musical needs.[15] In 1907, after the completion of a fine brick building and boasting an active congregation of four hundred baptized members, an Estey pipe organ was installed, the firm's op. 419, at a cost of $1,825, the funds raised by the young people of the congregation.[16] This congregation would become the mother

14 Arthur C. Repp, "Fedor, Lee County, Texas—Daughter of Serbin," *Concordia Historical Institute Quarterly*, Vol. 21, No. 2 (July 1948), available at https://forum.wendishresearch.org/viewthread.php?action=printable& fid=408&tid=2711 (accessed September 5, 2020).

15 Gotthilf Birkmann, "Church Historical Memoirs of Pastor Emeritus G. Birkmann," *Texas Distriktbote* (April 1926), trans. Ray Martens at https://wendishresearch.org/history-and-culture/people/rev-gotthilf -birkmann/april-1926-church-historical-memoirs-of-pastor-emeritus -g-birkmann/ (accessed September 4, 2020).

16 The Estey opus list, maintained by the Estey Organ Museum, lists the Zion organ ("German Lutheran Church") as op. 419. "Estey Pipe Organ

Figure 4.2 The Pfeffer organ at St. Michael's Catholic Church
in Starkenburg, Missouri, is said to be virtually identical to the
1891 Pfeffer at Holy Cross in Warda. (Source: Rosalind Mohnsen
and Earl L. Miller, organists, *A Pfeffer Odyssey*, LP, liner notes by
William Van Pelt from material supplied by Donald T. Petering et al.
[Richmond: Organ Historical Society, 1982]: record jacket.)

Figure 4.3 The day of dedication for the Pfeiffer organ at St. Paul Lutheran in Serbin, 1904. Gerhard Kilian sits at the console with an unnamed calcant (pumper). (Source: Texas Wendish Heritage Society Museum and Archives, photo #198.)

Figure 4.4 The Hinners organ at Trinity, Fedor, Texas. (Source: Courtesy of Jeremy Clifton.)

congregation of the Lutheran churches in North Texas, as it remains to this day.

Pipe organ installations continued throughout Texas. The Hinners organ installed at St. Paul's Lutheran in Austin in 1914 was the next to serve an LCMS church, while the Wendish church at Fedor, Trinity Lutheran, installed a single-manual, three-rank Hinners organ in 1920.[17] A similar Hinners organ of four ranks was installed at Christ Lutheran in Noack, Texas, another Wendish settlement, sometime after the church was built in 1916.[18] In Houston, Trinity Lutheran had been formed in 1879 as a breakaway LCMS congregation from Rev. Braun's First German Evangelical Lutheran Church. Trinity installed a Reuter organ, op. 72, in their landmark stone edifice in 1922 in a dedication service played by Prof. Karl Haase, dean of music at Concordia Teachers College, Seward, Nebraska.[19] The *Houston Post* notes that "the Walther league contributed $1000 toward the purchase fund of the organ, and the congregation in general

---

Opus List," Estey Organ Museum, https://www.esteyorganmuseum.org/wp-content/uploads/2020/03/Estey-Pipe-Organs-Opus-List-BP-rev-3-14-2020.pdf#:~:text=%20%20%20Title%20%20%20Estey%20Pipe,%20%20Created%20Date%20%20%202020150915113823Z%20 (accessed September 7, 2020).

17 Details about this organ were provided by Jack Wiederhold and Jeremy Clifton. The organ was renovated and enlarged by Buschbeck Organ Company in 1999, in which a 4 Principle and 2 Octave were added to enhance the organ's utility in hymn singing.

18 Information courtesy of Jack Wiederhold. It should be noted that Hinners Organ Company of Pekin, Illinois, specialized in providing workhorse instruments to small rural churches. A catalog builder, these stock instruments were usually shipped via railroad, complete with a professional installer. These sturdy instruments were usually three to five ranks of flutes and principals and normally mechanical action. One instrument familiar to this writer at the Nativity of the Blessed Virgin Mary Catholic Church in Cestohowa, Texas, has pneumatic pedal action. Even though the pedalboard is thirty notes, pipes were only provided for the lowest twelve, the remainder simply coupling from the manual. These shortcuts allowed the firm to keep costs low.

19 "K. L. Haase, Organist, Dies at 83," *Lincoln Star* (May 10, 1955): 5.

contributed the other $2500." The organ was a capstone to a music program that consists of "fine musical programs," with Prof. E. Schultze as the organist and the pastor, Rev. J. W. Behnken, future president of the LCMS, listed as the choir director.[20] Carl Halter, noted musician, professor, liturgical scholar, and administrator at Concordia Chicago, received his first call after graduation to Trinity, Houston, where he was a teacher and musician for a time during the 1930s.[21] Immanuel Lutheran in Giddings, Texas, in the heart of the Wendish counties, installed a Kilgen pipe organ in 1923. Accounting for subsequent pipe organs after this date becomes unwieldy due to the proliferation of congregations and their consequent pipe organs.

• • •

When Texas congregational histories were compiled, occasionally a memorable (or long) sermon is mentioned, but in general, the manner in which public worship was administered, of which music is a significant part, received little acknowledgment. This lacuna can be noticed even in Jan Kilian's extensive correspondence—there are significant liturgical performance practice issues that he simply never mentions. This is not, of course, because music and ritual were not occurring or he did not find them important; instead, it is likely because the hymns people sang on Sunday morning, the manner in which they sang them, and any ancillary niceties such as liturgies and organists were simply such a regular staple of their worship life that they warranted little mention. After all, one sang hymns and liturgy from a hymnal that would last a couple generations—why would this be of enough interest that these particularities be recorded? Indeed, that sacred music was so ingrained into a congregational culture resulted in a very

20 "New Pipe Organ Is Installed in Trinity Lutheran Church," *Houston Post* (July 17, 1922): 7.
21 Tim Halter, email to the author, February 21, 2020.

Figure 4.5 The Reuter organ at Trinity, Houston, Texas. (Source: "New Pipe Organ Is Installed in Trinity Lutheran Church," *Houston Post*, July 17, 1922.)

real lack of documentation. Would historians know as much about Wendish musical practices had the conflict among Teinert, Leubner, and Kilian not manifest itself in the way it did? The details were well documented because they represented a curious twist of history, something out of the ordinary. In most places, however, the clergy, choir directors, organists, and other lay musical leaders practiced their vocations without any special notice, with little documentation produced from their activities.

Texas churches suffered from their own unique challenges. By the mid-nineteenth century, some mainline churches in the eastern United States were celebrating 100- or even 150-year anniversaries, already amassing endowments upon which they still rely. Even though the LCMS itself was organized in 1847, after Texas had been admitted to the Union, the cities in the Midwest where the synod was centered were fairly advanced in terms of infrastructure and their economic ability to support immigrant communities. St. Louis had its beginnings in the 1760s, although it would not incorporate as a city until 1822. Texas churches, which were largely rural, lacked many of the resources from which churches in the east benefited, foremost of which were items necessary to music ministry. This, coupled with the fact that details of music ministry were often omitted from congregational histories, make a historical assessment difficult. An exploration of Lutheran liturgical practices in Texas must be expanded beyond simply the LCMS, as churches changed affiliations through time, allowing one to discern trends that would be applicable to all Lutheran churches, regardless of denomination.

Lutheran churches generally viewed congregational singing as the most important expression of sacred music. Records from the Texas Synod's St. John Lutheran Church in Paige, Texas, founded in 1884, demonstrate the importance of singing: "The first year after organization was a busy one for St. John's... [including] ordering hymnals and church benches, buying a piano and cistern and building an outhouse."[22] At this church at least, purchasing proper hymnals was seemingly as important as supplying the church with an outhouse and water! This history continues, "In 1891 the church organ was raffled off at 50 cents per ticket and Pastor Bunge was asked to buy a 'good, substantial organ' with the raffle money."[23] Zion Lutheran Church in Arneckeville, a German congregation of the Texas Synod founded in 1868 by St. Chrischona missionaries, of which Adam Sager was an early pastor, has had "at least seven organs ... whether any type of musical instruments were used in the earliest years we do not know. The first mention of an organ was the purchase of a Prince Organ for $133.35 on March 3, 1877. Several were purchased during the years following. At least one was donated from the home of one of the members."[24] This congregation in the early years may even have benefited from the small organ Sager brought over from Switzerland. Regardless, an organ, even if only a Prince brand harmonium, was crucial to leading congregational singing. In the absence of a teacher/musician, leading the hymnody fell to the pastor, some of whom were more suited to the task than others. At the German Lutheran Church in Round Top, Fayette County, Texas, one parishioner recalled in 1931, "When our church was first organized we had no organ. The Reverend Krapf was a fair musician; it was up to him to give the beginning note in the song. On one particular Sunday his first note was entirely too high; one by one the singers dropped out—they couldn't make it, but one valiant soul, Mother Brinker, kept up the struggle.... By superhuman effort she screeched out High

---

22 Doris Goerner Laake, *History of St. John Lutheran Church, Paige, TX* (Paige, TX: St. John Lutheran Church, 1979): 3.

23 Ibid.: 5. In this case, an organ was not "raffled off"; rather, a raffle was held to fund buying an organ!

24 *The History of Zion Evangelical Lutheran Church Arneckeville, DeWitte County, TX 1868–1982* (Arneckeville, TX: Zion Lutheran, 1982): 74.

C, and then sat down."[25] Such was the importance for some instrument to keep pitch in these rural parishes. Whether a violin or harmonium, simply being able to depend on a consistent pitch certainly aided singing.

Lutheran churches were generally averse to song leaders, always preferring an organ as soon as it could be obtained. However, as one of its first official acts, St. Paul Lutheran Church in Cave Creek, Texas, another Texas Synod congregation, in 1884 elected a Mr. A. Quindel as *Vorsänger*, or song leader, in the hopes that the "congregational singing might be improved."[26] The idea of a song leader may have come from the Methodist circuit riders who made significant inroads with the Germans in Central Texas, and of which Kilian was quite critical. In this case, the situation turned out poorly, as in 1891, "the *Vorsänger* resigned, for, no doubt, the arrangement had not proven to be very satisfactory. The Pastor then offered to move his 'Harmonium' into the church for the congregational singing. For the next four years Miss Auguste Herbert served as the organist and the singing was much improved."[27] It seems that the new measures of the Methodists were no match for a good harmonium! Significantly, a choir is never mentioned as a solution for addressing poor congregational singing.

Choirs and choral singing beyond congregational hymnody required decades to gain traction in Texas Lutheran churches. Jan Kilian never mentioned directing a choir as part of the Serbin cantor's duties, but he did find great utility in Carl Teinert's violin playing, an instrument that definitely found liturgical use in Texas. In these early days, the congregation was the choir, which, of course, reflects Lutheran liturgical theology. Returning to St. John's Lutheran in Paige, records indicate that "although the date of organization is unknown, the church

---

25 Frank, *German Organbuilder*: 16.
26 *St. Paul Lutheran Church*: 5.
27 Ibid.: 6.

choir was singing on Christmas, Easter, Reformation and other special occasions by 1904. . . . By 1912 the choir was singing every Sunday morning. At that time, church members purchased their own song books and were responsible for bringing them to each worship service."[28] This is probably illustrative on several levels. First, the church had matured into its second decade before it organized a choir. Second, the choir's main job was to highlight important festivals of the church year and was not at first integrated into regular weekly worship. Rather than treating choirs as a trained subset of the congregation whose main duty it was to lead the congregation's singing, the choir now tended to a more specialized type of music ministry, performing "numbers" for a captive audience. Finally, it was an amateur and volunteer organization, but as such even required a monetary outlay from each participant to purchase music. Rev. Sager's church in Arneckeville began a choir in 1890, again into its second decade of existence, of which "there were about 21 members in the choir in 1900 led by Pastor Herzig. Pastor Rapp played for and directed the choir after Pastor Herzig left Zion. . . . During this time, the choir sang very little during worship services, but practically all efforts were directed toward the presentation of musical programs and special occasions. On special days, cantatas . . . were sung."[29] Back at St. Paul in Cave Creek, in 1892, "Pastor Haag organized a church choir . . . some members still speak of the many times they went to the choir practice and of their singing for various events."[30] This early emphasis on choral "specials," rather than on a liturgical use, seems typical of Lutheran choirs up to World War II. Churches organized choirs to perform concerts or "cantatas" at special times, not differing greatly from the approach of

---

28 Laake, *History of St. John*: 7–8.
29 *History of Zion Evangelical*: 74.
30 Laake, *History of St. John*: 6.

the many secular choirs (*Sängervereine*) in which their singers often participated.

The German immigrants hailed from a musical culture, and their seeming lack of development in liturgical music should not be taken to imply that they were generally musically illiterate. Rather, they might simply have had a particular liturgical piety for what constituted appropriate church music. The new pastor at Zion Lutheran Church of Charlottenburg, Texas, Rev. Konzach, "came over from Germany, alone, and he could not speak English. Later he had his sweetheart come over from Germany to join him. She was an opera singer and very much out of place in Charlottenburg. Her very fine operatic solos, which she sang once in a while in church fell on ears unfamiliar with classical music."[31] Perhaps this story warrants a more nuanced approach. Were the Germans really that unfamiliar with historic Western art or classical music? William Owens writes of the Texas Germans in his *Tell Me a Story, Sing Me a Song*, "Germans, peasants or not, could read and write. They never had had to go through generations of illiteracy that was the heritage of countless Anglo-Texans. They had books and newspapers, songbooks and sheet music. They had musical instruments and systems of music. They formed *Sängerbünde and Sängervereine*, organizations in which people met to *practice* the songs of the *Heimatland*, whether folk or art, and to sing them in concerts."[32]

Indeed, German secular singing societies could be found throughout the Texas Hill Country by the later nineteenth century and even before that. The rugged Texas plains and forests might have required forsaking much sophisticated music making, but German folk and art music was imbued within

31 *History of Zion Lutheran Church of Charlottenburg, Wied, Lavaca County, TX* (self-pub., n.d.): 1.
32 William A. Owens, *Tell Me a Story, Sing Me a Song: A Texas Chronicle* (Austin: University of Texas Press, 2011): 200.

many of the German Texans. It may be, however, that they had a clearer sense of what constituted *sacred* music, and operatic arias were not it. Perhaps the Charlottenburg pastor should have known better than to purvey his wife's opera arias on a congregation expecting Lutheran sacred music. Gerald Frank contends that these early Texas Lutherans had been formed to appreciate all manner of music: "It is apparent, therefore, that the German immigrants retained music making and music education among their priorities, even though the conditions for the same could not have been as highly developed as in their fatherland. Music was used in divine services and was taught to children. The precise nature of the music for the services and of the liturgies in which it was used—not to mention the standards of the same—remain questions today."[33] One must sympathize with these early Texans. Although there is a tendency to romanticize their church music situation in Europe, certainly at least some immigrants had experienced enough dramatic Lutheran music and liturgy to have carried that ideal in their ears to Texas, where their celebration of the Word and Sacrament would no longer benefit from such enrichments. Acquiring an organ of some type was the first step in fulfilling this vision, followed next by a stable choir. These developments usually took decades and represented a multigenerational commitment to the church.

---

33 Frank, *German Organbuilder*: 17.

5

Lutheran Sacred Music in the Heart of Texas

The LCMS may have endured an inauspicious, yet faithful, entry into Texas through the ministry of Rev. Jan Kilian among the Wends. Kilian understood the necessity of affiliating with what he perceived to be an orthodox synod in the new land, as much as he might have longed for some of the civilization, established tradition, and ecclesiastical order of the Saxon and Prussian churches. Certainly, joining the LCMS was a bit of a concession for him, and his relationship with St. Louis waxed and waned through three decades, the strain sometimes a result of the lack of communication and travel difficulties, which simply enhanced the loneliness to which Kilian had already tended. His was not to be a ministry of direct influence outside of the Wends. The Wendish people established their towns generally away from others—even from other Wends—in what was certainly an exemplar of that rugged individualism that the state of Texas seemed to be able to draw from its settlers. Texas attracted all manner of people who were of an independent mindset, or who learned to become so. Yet the Wends were a minority within a minority, their language and customs seeming strange even to the German speakers in Texas. Their liturgy and their singing style differed from that of their German brethren, a contentious issue in Serbin itself, leading to fraction and discord through the years. Yet the heritage of faithful Lutheranism Kilian nurtured would soon find expression and flourish beyond the Wendish settlements.

Founding St. Paul Lutheran, Austin

In 1891, a few stalwart Lutheran settlers in Austin, the heart and capital of Texas, persuaded the board of missions of the southern district of the LCMS to establish a congregation in the city, with Rev. Hermann Kilian, Jan's son, serving as mission pastor.[1] Hermann, assisted by other pastors from Lee County as well as his brother Gerhard, would shepherd the small flock for the first year before they were able to call their first pastor. The first building was dedicated in 1893, with Hermann returning to preach at that service; the congregation began a school that same year, teaching in both English and German.[2] Otherwise, the liturgies and business affairs of the church were conducted in German until 1898, when Rev. J. H. Tegeler instituted an English service. In 1904, the congregation constructed a new church, which itself was replaced in 1913 by a yet larger sanctuary, seating as many as three hundred. Hermann returned to preach at the dedication service of this new $10,000 church at the corner of Sixteenth and Red River Streets.[3] Having served since 1906, Rev. Karl George Manz was assisted in musical ministry in the early years by Professor F. W. Bopp, who, although not listed in the church records as a called teacher, must have come from a notable family in the church, as he also had assisted in drawing up the plans for the 1913 building. In April 1906, the congregation

---

1 "St. Paul's Lutheran Church," *Austin Daily Statesman* (January 19, 1913): 83.
2 Ibid.
3 "Germans Dedicate New Church on Red River," *Austin Daily Statesman* (December 1, 1913): 3.

Figure 5.1 St. Paul Lutheran Church. (Source: "Handsome Lutheran Church Erected at Cost of $10,000," *Austin American*, May 21, 1916.)

voted to purchase an "Agenda" and to sing the congregational responses in the liturgy, suggesting they had not done so before.[4] Rev. Manz, as the two pastors prior to him had, taught in the school, but recent growth had necessitated that the congregation call a teacher.

That the congregation called a teacher with musical proclivities is of no particular consequence, for they were all trained for certain musical competencies; however, the candidate, Ernst Thuernau, must have excelled musically, developing a reputation for organ performance on the church's $1,200 Hinners

---

4 "History of the First Fifty Years," 1991, personal files of Kathy Achterberg, former director of music at St. Paul.

organ installed in 1914, the year of Thuernau's arrival.[5] Born
in Craig, Missouri, in 1894, little is known about Thuernau's
early life and education, but he would have been twenty years
old in 1914 when he arrived at St. Paul as a teacher and parish
musician,[6] old enough to have completed a course of study at
one of the synodical schools, possibly in St. Louis.[7] At a 1915
mission festival, the *Austin American-Statesman* noted that
"the beauty of the services was enhanced by special music by
the organist, Prof. E Thuernau, at every service. Some of these
special numbers were: 'Cradle Song,' by Delbrueck; largo [sic]
from 'Xerses,' by Handel, and 'Traumerei,' by Schumann."[8]
This repertoire, unremarkable as it is, represents the fashion of
the era and a preference for pastiche pieces rather than actual
organ music and sacred literature. By 1916, Thuernau had
established a men's choir that, for confirmation in April of that
year, sang "Savior Who Thy Flock Are Feeding"; Thuernau led
a "catechumen's choir" that same day singing "Take Thou My
Hand and Lead Me."[9] By 1916, he had accepted a call to Zion
Lutheran in St. Louis, where he was a staple of community life
until a few years before his death, leading the four-hundred-
voice Lutheran Choirs of Greater St. Louis as well as directing
a comprehensive music ministry at Zion. He must have been a
performer of some renown, as he returned to Austin in 1917
to play an organ recital at St. Paul.[10] Another visit to Austin in
July 1923 saw him perform again, perhaps demonstrating the

---

5 Ibid.
6 Ernst Thuernau's death certificate, Division of Health of Missouri,
   March 1, 1955.
7 The Lutheran *Statistical Yearbook* of 1912, during which time he would
   have been in college, lists his address as "Baldwin, Ill.," a small town
   outside of St. Louis.
8 "St. Paul's Lutherans Hold Mission Festival at Church," *Austin American* (November 22, 1915): 5.
9 "Class of Eight Confirmed at Lutheran Church," *Austin American*
   (April 10, 1916): 6.
10 "News of Churches," *Statesman* (Austin, TX; September 1, 1917): 8.

congregation's early commitment to music. The paper writes of this recital: "E. H. Thuerman [*sic*], organist and choirmaster of Zion's Lutheran Church, St Louis, MO. appeared in his second organ recital in Austin on Sunday night under the auspices of the local Walther League. His organ numbers were very much enjoyed by a large audience. He also gave three vocal selections, being accompanied by Carl A. Fehr. From here he will go to Houston, Texas, where he will give a recital at Trinity Lutheran Church."[11]

That Thuernau performed in Houston as well suggests that he was well known even after only two years in the state and that he could certainly be counted among the better organists regionally. This also suggests an approbation of "secular" recitals within church buildings, certainly an idea not even uniformly accepted today. Thuernau returned to Texas at least once more for another concert in July 1926, the paper acclaiming him as "a very good player of the pipe organ." This program included "Jubilate" by Ralph Kinder, "Caprice" by Sheldon, "Concert Fantasia" by Diggle, "Sortie" by Davis, and "Variations on 'Wait on God'" by Ryan as well as "vocal numbers" including "Sicher in Jesu Armen," "sung by the soloist as a memorial to the sainted teacher, G. A. Killian."[12] Gerhard Kilian had died in 1916, at the end of Thuernau's tenure, but along with his brother Hermann, he seemed to stay connected with St. Paul, even after other clergy and teachers had come along. Gerhard, of course, had studied at the Addison Teachers' Seminary, played organ in Serbin, and spent some of his final years in Austin, where he died.[13] Thuernau was followed as the teacher and parish musician by H. Schumacher, while Oscar

---

11 "Thurnau Pleases Large Audience," *Austin American-Statesman* (July 10, 1923): 5.

12 "Organ Recital at St. Paul's Church," *Austin American-Statesman* (July 25, 1926): 18.

13 "Obituary: G. A. Kilian," *Austin American-Statesman* (September 13, 1916): 6.

Thoreson played organ with the aforementioned Carl Fehr, a teenager of whom more will be said later, assisting on occasion.

Thus, St. Paul, as the mother church of the Austin-area LCMS, early established itself with active educational and musical ministries. At the congregation's initiative and with early financial support, the Lutheran Concordia College would be founded nearby in 1926, its main building, Kilian Hall, paying homage to Jan Kilian and that family's contributions to the Texas LCMS. The saga of Lutheran Concordia College and the history of St. Paul parish are so inexorably intertwined—between their shared faculty, musicians, facilities, and for many years, a partly collective vision—that their impact on Lutheran sacred music in Texas needs to be considered together.

Addison Teachers' Seminary

For two reasons, the Addison Teachers' Seminary, the first institution of what is now the Concordia University system, needs to be considered before returning to Texas Lutheran musical concerns. First, the Illinois teachers college would establish a certain educational model in which music was integral, a model followed by later institutions with some variation, thus justifying a brief analysis of the curriculum, faculty, and practices of this seminary. Second, Addison would teach many of the teachers and parish musicians in Texas in these early years, the first being Gerhard Kilian, whose musical education there would position him at the forefront of early Texan Lutheran church musicians. Although, due to a fire in 1914 that destroyed the early records, it cannot be determined exactly how many Texas church musicians and teachers had received their early training in Addison, anecdotal evidence suggests a considerable number were sent to Texas, their musical training in Illinois informing their musical practices in their new parishes.

Concordia Teachers' College, Addison, Ill. Built in 1864

Figure 5.2 The Addison Teachers' Seminary. (Source: Warren Schmidt, "Grosse Kirchen-Part 2," Perry County Historical Society, posted April 16, 2019, https://lutheranmuseum.com/2019/04/16/grosse-kirchen-part-2/.)

Founded in 1864, only the synodical seminaries antedated the Addison school, which was "devoted exclusively to teacher training,"[14] later relocating to Chicago as Concordia Teachers College, now Concordia Chicago. Although called a "seminary," its students were prepared for teaching in the synod's parish schools rather than for ordination, although pastoral ministry was certainly a route many graduates chose to take and for which the curriculum prepared them well. In an era in which most LCMS parishes either supported a parochial school or harbored designs to do so, the synod realized the value of a uniquely Lutheran education for its teachers: "One of the biggest

---

14 Alfred Freitag, *College with a Cause: A History of Concordia Teachers College* (River Forest, IL: Concordia Teachers College, 1966): 3.

problems was that of maintaining the ratio of one school for each congregation. The shortage of teachers was so great that in the earlier years of the Synod most pastors also had to teach. As the church grew, constantly redoubling its efforts to reach the thousands upon thousands of German immigrants who entered our country toward the middle of the 19th century, it was simply impossible to find enough manpower to serve them all and to provide Christian education for their children."[15] Indeed, much of Jan Kilian's stress had resulted from attempting to balance teaching and pastoral obligations, eventually relieved when his son returned to Serbin as a teacher. This same consideration certainly motivated Rev. Manz in Austin to call a full-time teacher. In that parish, the two preceding pastors had also served as teachers, an increasingly untenable situation as the congregation grew. Pedagogy at Addison was steeped in Lutheran doctrine and practice, and intentionally so. The education offered in the "normal," or teaching, schools of the era not only lacked Christocentricity but also offered scant training in the classics, a dearth this early Lutheran institution was able successfully to fill, whereby, according to Alfred Freitag, "Its curriculum was generally in advance of the normal-school program then in existence."[16] Music, of course, was an integral element of the classical education this Lutheran institution sought to convey.

The education offered at Addison Teachers' Seminary was initially inspired by the German *Gymnasium* model of education through which many of its founders had matriculated. As such, a boy (in the early days, this education was offered only to males) would commence his five-year residential studies around age sixteen, the first three years roughly equivalent to high school, with a final two years of preprofessional training, akin to junior college. As a classical institution, the

15 Ibid.: 35.
16 Ibid.: 22.

seminary maintained lofty goals: "Besides being well qualified in the schoolroom, the Lutheran teacher was expected to
be proficient in music, including choir conducting, piano,
organ, and violin, so that he could teach music to the school-
children and lead congregational singing in church services.
The violin was often the only instrument available to teach and
lead singing."[17] Rather than viewing musical study as a tangential adjunct to the core curriculum, the faculty emphasized
music in the context of the classical quadrivium. An 1869 class
schedule for three faculty at the Addison school (at the time
Gerhard Kilian would have been in attendance) evidences that
Karl Brauer, professor of music, taught thirty-three periods of
music a week, in contrast to Professor Selle, who taught only
twenty-seven periods in the general liberal arts, although of
these, even thirteen of Selle's periods were devoted to teaching piano. In contrast, President Lindemann taught twenty-six
nonmusic class periods. In this weekly schedule, the musical
instruction was divided as follows:

Singing: five periods   Organ: seven periods
Violin: five periods   Music theory: one period[18]
Piano: twenty-eight
    periods

It is likely that one could "place out" of certain musical instruction, as "a considerable number of students during the beginning years of the seminary were not only older but also quite well
educated, and in many cases they did not even need additional

---

17 Ibid. Recall that Carl Teinert was noted for his violin playing in Serbin,
   also suggesting its prevalent use as a liturgical instrument. The violin
   was easily portable and also relatively easy to learn, at least if one needed
   only to learn the melodies in the hymnal, both of which would have been
   substantial advantages on the prairies of Texas.
18 Ibid.: 48.

instruction in music."[19] The seminary's first president, Johann Christoph Wilhelm Lindemann (himself a relative of Martin Luther), suggested that a teacher must be proficient in music, and it seems that qualification extended to his faculty at least to some degree, given that Selle had to teach thirteen periods of piano. In the *Schulblatt* (the journal of the school) of August 1868, Lindemann asks "what is required of a teacher," to which he responds (1) possessing Christian character; (2) having knowledge of English and German; (3) demonstrating good ability in math, singing, and playing piano, organ, and violin; and (4) fulfilling that scriptural standard, being "apt to teach."[20]

A choir, an ad hoc sort of ensemble, was organized the first year and sang twice the second semester at the churches of Rodenberg and Schaumberg, the choir having to "walk there on Saturday, stay overnight, and walk back Sunday night, tired and dusty."[21] The first buildings were primitive and the facilities initially inadequate for some of the seminary's aspirations, which probably mitigated against the organization of formal choirs in the early years, although the aforementioned chorus "was called on many times over the years for special music at church. In 1866 a small choir was organized just before Christmas. On New Year's Eve they went caroling at the homes of residents."[22] Although one cannot be certain from the paucity of materials that speak to the situation directly, it seems as though *sacred music*, or music "at church," bore pride of place. In 1881, the synodical convention clarified entrance requirements such that "the entrant should be able to sing alone and correctly such melodies as are being sung in his church nearly every Sunday";[23] thus, the music curriculum endeavored not to fashion

---

19 Ibid.: 92.
20 Ibid.: 49.
21 Ibid.: 45.
22 Ibid.: 101.
23 Ibid.: 64.

musical performers of the concert repertoire, who could render a Schubert Lied to perfection, but rather to form teachers who could execute sacred music with a requisite satisfying proficiency. The Addison seminary was not a conservatory, but its musical instruction must have ranked fairly highly, at least at times, given the standard of some of the faculty and students.

After a certain Wilhelm F. Hoffmann, who had taught music part time during the first two years, took a call to Milwaukee, the synod authorized in the autumn of 1866 the calling of teacher Karl Brauer as a full-time professor of music.[24] An immigrant who only had been in the United States since 1850, Brauer was born on January 10, 1831, in Lisberg, Hessen, graduating from the Friedberg Teachers' Seminary. He taught at St. Johns, Philadelphia (1850–54); Trinity, St. Louis (1854–55); Zion, Cleveland (1855–65); and Trinity, Baltimore (1865–66), where he was apparently dismissed for insisting to teach Luther's *Catechism*.[25] According to Carl Schalk, Brauer "was the first prominent music instructor in the Missouri Synod. His writings include many articles on music, organs, and organ playing which appeared in the *Ev-Luth. Schulblatt*."[26] Brauer's *Mehrstimmiges Choralbuch* of 1888 probably stands as his most enduring contribution, containing as it does harmonizations to all the hymns in Walther's hymnal of 1847, favoring the original rhythmic versions of the chorales "for future pastors, cantors, and organists . . . to put into the hands of those who are preparing themselves for such service the most complete collection possible which they can afterwards use in the

---

24 Ibid.: 47.

25 William Herman Theodore Dau, *Ebenezer: Reviews of the Work of the Missouri Synod during Three Quarters of a Century* (St. Louis, MO: Concordia, 1922): 205, 218.

26 Carl Schalk, *Source Documents in American Lutheran Hymnody* (St. Louis, MO: CPH, 1996): 90.

Prof. Carl Brauer.

Figure 5.3 Karl Brauer, professor of music at the Addison Seminary,
the first notable music professor in the LCMS. (Source: W. H. Dau,
ed., *Ebenezer: Reviews of the Work of the Missouri Synod during Three
Quarters of a Century* [St. Louis, MO: CPH, 1922]: 218.)

service of the congregation."[27] Brauer retired from Addison in
1897 and died in 1907.

In 1871, Brauer had announced in *Der Lutheraner* that a
new organ, made by J. G. Pfeffer of St. Louis, had been acquired
by the school. According to Brauer, this ten-rank, two-manual

---

27 Ibid.: 89.

organ with a twenty-seven-note pedal division "offered the softest to the loudest of voices," and he anticipated "that the organ could be used for both church services and for teaching."[28] During his tenure, another unspecified organ and piano were purchased in 1881,[29] with a new pipe organ for the chapel built in 1890 by Carl Barkhoff of Salem, Ohio, who altruistically absorbed much of the expense himself.[30] Whether there was a pipe organ at the seminary before the Pfeffer of 1871 is unknown, but at least they had access to a harmonium with a pedalboard, as Gerhard Kilian learned to play organ pedals during his years in Addison (he graduated in 1872). Brauer must have taught hundreds of students during his three decades at the seminary, and one can only lament that his contributions have not been studied further.

Underscoring the importance of music within the curriculum, the synod authorized an additional professor of music in 1879, with John Merkel assuming the interim position until 1881, when a call was issued to Ernest Homann, a Chicago teacher who "was known as a very proficient pianist."[31] Professor Albert Kaeppel, formerly of Trinity, St. Louis, was appointed in 1897 to replace Brauer.[32] Kaeppel deserves mention, as he taught at Addison until his death in 1934. With Rev. Paul Kretzmann as librettist, Kaeppel composed the music in 1921 for a Christmas cantata entitled "Unto Us," and he seems to have been a formidable performer as well. For a 1908 organ dedication in Rock Island, Illinois, Kaeppel, "one of the foremost organists in the country" according to the local paper, could be found playing Bach's Toccata in F-Major, the "Allegretto in B-Minor" of Guilmant, the "Spring Song"

---

28 Karl Brauer, "Die neue Orgel in unserem Schullehrer Seminar," *Der Lutheraner* (St. Louis, MO; October 15, 1869): 31.

29 Freitag, *College with a Cause*: 63.

30 Ibid.: 68.

31 Ibid.: 62.

32 Dau, *Ebenezer*: 221.

of Hollins, an unspecified Mendelssohn sonata, and a "Choral Fantasia" of his own composition.[33] These are more significant works from the organ literature than many of his contemporaries were playing. The seminary produced at least one seasoned concert organist and likely many more fine organists of lesser magnitude. One such performer is Edward Rechlin, son of Addison's Professor Frederick Rechlin, who taught at Addison from 1893 until his death in 1915.[34] Born in 1884, Edward Rechlin graduated from the Addison seminary, studying with Kaeppel and performing at the St. Louis World's Fair in 1904, after which he continued his studies with Alexandre Guilmant and Charles-Marie Widor in France. A performer of national repute based in New York City, "Rechlin's early involvement with music grew out of a German Lutheran tradition that linked the roles of organist and choirmaster with the office of Christian teacher, often in parochial schools."[35] Rechlin is perhaps the exception that proves the rule: the Addison seminary sought to produce competent teachers who could serve as respectable organists and choir directors—not concert performers but liturgical musicians who could play a service adequately. The model is one that produced not exciting performers but rather competent musicians who could serve in the field in Texas, for example, whether playing a pedal harmonium or a modest pipe organ.

33　"To Dedicate Lutheran Church Organ," *Rock Island Argus* (Rock Island, IL; July 25, 1908): 6.

34　Freitag, *College with a Cause*, appendix A.

35　Victor Gebauer, "Edward Rechlin," Center for Church Music, Concordia Chicago, https://www.cuchicago.edu/globalassets/images/center-for -church-music/profiles/center-for-church-music---profiles---rechlin .pdf (accessed January 21, 2022).

Lutheran Concordia College, Austin

At the instigation of Rev. Manz and St. Paul parish, the synod established this new college, with *Lutheran* preceding *Concordia* in the name so as to differentiate this institution from masonic organizations who also utilized *Concordia* nomenclature. The cornerstone of Kilian Hall, named after the revered founder of the LCMS in Texas, was laid on June 27, 1926, to great ceremony and with the accompaniment of "the orchestra of St. Paul's Lutheran church in Austin, and the band of the Lutheran church at Walburg," suggesting some of the musical forces these congregations were able to muster, at least for important occasions.[36] The new Lutheran college, within two miles' proximity to St. Paul, would be modeled after its predecessor schools, not only Addison (which at this point had moved to River Forest), but also the other Concordias that had been established within the last forty years. The synod paid a portion of the college's expenses, allowing a historical paper trail starting in 1926, in which the synod approved a "voucher" for a music teacher at the school.[37] Structured in the *Gymnasium* manner consistent with the other colleges, the first faculty included a professor of music—in this case, Ewald F. Wilkening.[38]

Whether the letter approving a music teacher at the school refers to the position eventually held by Wilkening is unknown, but it is likely. Born in 1891, Wilkening had graduated from the Addison Teachers' Seminary in 1910, probably studying

---

36 "Lutherans to Lay College Cornerstone Sunday Afternoon," *Austin American-Statesman* (June 27, 1926): 1.

37 William Hagen, letter to Rev. R. Osthoff, December 29, 1926 (University of North Texas Libraries, Portal to Texas History), https://texashistory.unt.edu/ark:/67531/metapth591380/ (accessed September 1, 2020).

38 See Concordia University faculty, untitled photograph, n.d. (University of North Texas Libraries, Portal to Texas History), https://texashistory.unt.edu/ark:/67531/metapth20117/m1/1/?q=concordia%20university (accessed August 26, 2020).

Figure 5.4 Kilian Hall, the primary living/teaching space of Lutheran Concordia College in Austin, at its dedication in 1926. (Source: Killian Hall dedication service, October 17, 1926 [University of North Texas Libraries, Portal to Texas History], https://texashistory.unt.edu/ark:/67531/metapth20121/ [accessed February 2, 2022].)

organ with Professor Kaeppel. He served as a teacher at Salem Lutheran in Malone, Texas, from 1910 to 1920, at which time he was called to St. Paul in Austin, serving as the principal, teacher, and parish musician. At his installation as the "organist and parochial school teacher," the Walther League performed a program of vocal and piano music to welcome him, promising him pleasant years ahead.[39] Indeed, that he continued in the position until 1957 suggests a fruitful, happy environment, and he must have had a collegial relationship with Rev. Manz; a newspaper clipping from August 12, 1923, alerts the community that "there shall be no church on Sunday" because the pastor and organist would be in Giddings, preaching and playing for the installation of a new pipe organ.[40] That Wilkening was invited to play this dedication intimates that by this time, he had ranked as one of the foremost Lutheran organists in Texas in one of the most

---

39 "Obituary: E. F. Wilkening," *Austin Statesman* (June 19, 1963): 6.
40 "News of the Churches," *Austin Statesman* (August 12, 1923): 27.

Figure 5.5 Teacher Ewald F. Wilkening, longtime principal, organist, and educator at St. Paul, and the first instructor in music at Concordia. (Source: *Blue Bonnet*, yearbook of Concordia Lutheran College, Austin, TX, 1930 [University of North Texas Libraries, Portal to Texas History], https://texashistory.unt.edu/ark:/67531/metapth639209/ [accessed February 2, 2022]: 14.)

influential churches in the Texas LCMS. His support from the church must have continued even after he accepted the part-time responsibility for "music and choir" at the college in 1926. That he was able to teach at the college and still manage his parish duties at St. Paul speaks to the importance the congregation placed on the new school and their willingness to give sacrificially of their called workers' time, not to mention the importance they placed on music in spiritual formation. (Rev. Manz also served on the college's board of control.)

Early musical endeavors at Concordia included the vocal Octet, whose efforts in 1930 "were devoted chiefly to the study of sacred music and in particular Lutheran Hymns."[41] Although a "lack of material and training proved the severest barriers," the choir "rendered frequent Sacred Concerts in the neighboring congregations. The Easter holidays marked a successful tour into northern Texas. We can with confidence say that the programs were highly appreciated by the audiences reached. In fostering the study and rendition of sacred music the octet has not only added to the laurels of our Alma Mater but has also afforded each member invaluable training in this art."[42] This description is perhaps telling in that this modest ensemble is no glee club, although that would come about with its own purpose; rather, the Octet sought to learn sacred music and perform it regionally. This is not a novel concept today, as the spring tour is a feature of many college bands and choirs, but at this time, they would have provided music for small country churches whose music program consisted perhaps solely of a self-taught organist.

Personalities and Pedagogy

A report from February 1929 from Concordia president H. Studtmann offers clues as to the basic musical curriculum in the first few years of the school's existence: "At this institution during the first year . . . Mr. Carl Fehr gave musical instruction. Teacher F. Wilkening gave singing instruction. In the second year . . . Teacher Wilkening taught music and singing. This last year we had four teachers . . . Teacher Wilkening again gave music and singing instruction."[43]

---

41 *Blue Bonnet*, yearbook of Concordia Lutheran College, Austin, TX, 1930 (University of North Texas Libraries, Portal to Texas History), https:// texashistory.unt.edu/ark:/67531/metapth639209/ (accessed September 1, 2020): 30.

42 Ibid.

43 H. Studtmann, letter to "Vorsitzer," February 20, 1929 (University of North Texas Libraries, Portal to Texas History), https://texashistory.unt

Figure 5.6 The Octet, the premiere choral ensemble of Lutheran Concordia College, was dedicated to promulgating sacred music. Pictured here is the 1930 ensemble. (Source: *Blue Bonnet*, yearbook of Concordia Lutheran College, Austin, TX, 1930 [University of North Texas Libraries, Portal to Texas History], https://texashistory.unt.edu/ark:/67531/metapth639209/ [accessed February 2, 2022]: 25.)

A member of a prominent church family, Carl Fehr had grown up and been formed in the music ministry at St. Paul for a number of years, but likely due to his own studies, his contribution to the college seemed to be limited to the first year, and Wilkening seems to have taken up musical instruction as well as vocal instruction. Vocal instruction probably means literally "private voice lessons" or "singing instructions" rather than "chorus," which in this era seems only to have been the Octet. This chorus seems to have been led, at least in 1928 and 1929, by Reinhold Zwintscher,[44] a young instructor of Greek who

.edu/ark:/67531/metapth606593/ (accessed September 1, 2020).
44 "Reinhold Zwintscher," Findagrave.com, https://www.findagrave.com/memorial/98995744/reinhold-r_-zwintscher (accessed August 1, 2020).

intended to enter the St. Louis seminary in September 1930. Zwintscher, having led the Octet on a successful tour through Texas the previous year, "was planning a more extensive one next spring." However, during a trip home to Plato, Minnesota, in December 1929, Zwintscher developed pneumonia and died on Christmas Day, responding to which "the faculty of the college, the Concordia octette, and St. Paul's Lutheran church will honor Mr. Zwintscher by presenting three memorial wreathes at the burial."[45] It seems, for one, that Wilkening was not in charge of the chorus and that, as a matter of principle, chorus, musical theory, and singing classes were all offered separately by different faculty, at least in these years in question. Also notable is that Zwintscher's primary teaching focus was Greek rather than music, suggesting the comprehensive training of the synod's teaching colleges, of which Zwintscher was certainly a graduate. His classical education had prepared him to teach Greek . . . and lead a chorus.[46] At this early stage in the college's development, there was no full-time music instructor.

Musical instruction would have presented many more difficulties had St. Paul not been able to offer the support of its staff, in this case at least Fehr and Wilkening, who need not have depended on the school to provide them a living. A curious correspondence from March 1930 from M. F. Kretzmann, secretary of the synod, suggests just how much control the synod maintained on the college, which was far from self-supporting, even to the point of involvement in setting the wages for musical faculty: "At its last meeting the Board of Directors took up the question whether the $200 extra for singing lessons should be paid to our professors, in case that they happen to give these extra lessons. Originally this rule applied only to school teachers who were employed for such extra work. Our Board ruled that such extra remuneration should be given to one of our

---

45 "R. Zwintscher," *Austin American* (December 28, 1929): 2.
46 No record can be found indicating where Zwintscher attended school.

professors who happens to do this extra work, especially now, since Synod has raised the salary of our instructors."[47] Ewald Wilkening was certainly the faculty in question, as he would have been the only person offering vocal instruction that year. This raises some ancillary questions that perhaps cannot be answered fully. If there was such great interest in singing lessons from the student body, why not a second chorus, a "choral union," to supplement the elite, auditioned Octet? Did the singers walk over to St. Paul to sing in Teacher Wilkening's church choir? If so, one can easily envision the situation arising that singers from his own choir—who might happen to be Concordia students—would request singing instruction, perhaps outside of regular studies. Would he be compensated by the student or the school/synod? The indistinct boundaries between the parish and the academy here present a bit of problem but, in general, demonstrate that an integrated spiritual life—with sacred music "next to the Word of God" in importance—was the goal of Lutheran higher education and that minor practical issues would intrude on occasion.

In these early years, St. Paul parish and neighboring Concordia College shared staff, facilities, and even a common vision. By 1931, Carl Fehr had been called as a teacher to St. Paul, likely to assist Wilkening, whose original called duties of "organist and teacher" had by now expanded to principal. The Fehr family had long connections in Texas Lutheranism. Carl's maternal grandfather was Gerhard Kilian, while Carl's father, Herman, a barber and businessman of some note in the city and member of St. Paul, had been involved with Pastor Manz and Ewald Wilkening in establishing Concordia.[48] Born

---

47 M. F. Kretzmann, letter to R. Osthoff, March 26, 1930 (University of North Texas Libraries, Portal to Texas History), https://texashistory.unt .edu/ark:/67531/metapth606588/ (accessed September 1, 2020).

48 "Austin May Get $150,000 College, Fehr Says," *Austin Statesman* (July 16, 1924): 6.

on November 29, 1907, in Austin, the younger Fehr received his BA from the University of Texas in 1928 and his MA in 1930. He then graduated from Concordia Teachers College in River Forest in 1931, after which he received an official call to teach at St. Paul.[49] (Fehr's teaching at Concordia, then, had been during his undergraduate days.) During his brief tenure as a teacher at St. Paul, he actively developed the music program, ostensibly leaving Wilkening more time to devote to his duties as principal. By 1930, St. Paul had a junior choir,[50] which, at least in December of that year, was directed by Carl Fehr, whose father at the time was serving as the Sunday school superintendent.[51] In December 1930, Wilkening is still listed as the official organist and choir director in newspaper reports, but by 1932, only Fehr is listed in that position, although both Wilkening and Studtmann, president of Concordia, were singing in Fehr's choir. An advertisement for a Christmas cantata at St. Paul in 1932 provides a glimpse into the music ministry as it developed under Fehr:

> The Christmas cantata, "Noel," by Henry Wessel will be presented by the senior and junior choirs of St. Paul's Lutheran Church. . . . Carl A. Fehr is choir director and organist.
>
> The junior choir, organized about four years ago, was the first vested choir in the Missouri Synod of Lutheran churches in Texas and other churches in the state have now organized similar choirs.[52]

The paper then proceeds to list a senior choir of seven sopranos, five altos, four tenors, and five basses. The junior choir

---

49 "Miss Knippa Weds Carl A. Fehr Here," *Austin American* (June 5, 1933): 3.
50 "Austin Church Services Sunday," *Austin Statesman* (March 8, 1930): 8.
51 "Sunday Services in Austin Churches," *Austin American* (December 20, 1930): 6.
52 "Cantata at St. Paul's Planned," *American Statesman* (December 25, 1932): 7.

consisted of twenty girls divided into soprano and alto *divisi*. This is the first notice of a "vested" junior choir, which, if established around 1928, would have been during Wilkening's tenure, although Fehr likely started the choir himself when he was involved with the church on a volunteer basis.[53]

Interestingly, Carl Fehr's older brother, Arthur, was a noted architect who in his early days had assisted in the design of Concordia's main building, Kilian Hall, eponymously named after his own great-grandfather. Arthur achieved great heights in his career, and Carl must have been no less ambitious. In the summer of 1934, First Methodist Church in Austin appointed Carl as its organist and director of music,[54] but only three years later, he assumed a similar position at St. David's Episcopal Church.[55] He would remain at St. David's while energetically pursuing a career directing high school and university glee clubs until 1945, when he was appointed as the assistant professor of music at the College of William and Mary in Williamsburg, Virginia.[56] Eventually receiving a doctorate in music education from Columbia, Carl would retire as the chancellor professor of music at William and Mary, having been "recognized by the Freedoms Foundation in 1969 and was named one of the outstanding music educators in the country in 1971."[57] Perhaps Carl's illustrious career stands as a testimony to his Kilian family legacy and the Wendish culture so steeped in sacred and folk music as well as to the nurturing environment

53 "Austin Choral Director Takes New Position," *Austin American* (June 3, 1945): 11.

54 "Carl Fehr Named Director of Music," *Austin American* (July 14, 1934): 6.

55 "St. David's Has New Schedule," *Austin American* (June 5, 1937): 12.

56 "Carl Fehr, Who Will Teach in Virginia, Gives Recital," *Austin American* (August 30, 1945): 7.

57 "Obituary: Carl A. Fehr," *Austin American-Statesman* (April 21, 1994): 31.

fostered by the Lutherans at St. Paul and Concordia for the many opportunities they offered.

Returning the subject to St. Paul and Austin, Teacher Gustave Leonard (Ben) Bentrup offered some long-term stability to the parish music ministry, serving from 1933 to 1943.[58] Bentrup graduated from Concordia Teachers College in River Forest and continued his studies at Southwest Texas Teachers College in San Marcos, Texas. He was an "instructor in music in Concordia academy, choir instructor and director in St. Paul's Lutheran school."[59]

The arrival of John Socha in August 1944 heralds the story of one of the more colorful personalities of the era. Born in 1919 of Czechoslovakian heritage in Garfield, New Jersey, Socha graduated from Concordia, River Forest, in December 1940, where he was the "captain of the football team and edited the college paper. He has also been active in youth work. He was recently re-elected president of the western district of the Lutheran league [sic], and until recently edited the district youth publications."[60] Upon graduation, he served St. John Lutheran Church in Park Forest, Illinois.[61] He was subsequently encouraged by Texas native, former Texas District president, and by then synod president Rev. Dr. J. W. Behnken to "accept a teacher-musician position at St. Paul Lutheran School in Austin."[62] According to Socha, "Dr. Behnken told me that Texas was both a pioneer state and a frontier for me."[63] This suggests, perhaps, that still in the 1940s, synod leadership viewed Texas as a wild

58 "Frankie Vivian Bentrup," Findagrave.com, https://www.findagrave .com/memorial/182028880/frankie-vivian-bentrup (accessed August 20, 2020).

59 "Shower Fete Is Friday Event," *American-Statesman* (June 2, 1940): 27.

60 Barbara Holsomback, "He's a Pastor for All Seasons," *Fort Worth Star Telegram* (June 22, 1977): 17.

61 "History of the First Fifty Years."

62 Ibid.

63 Ibid.

frontier with only a few beacons of Lutheranism shining forth, by then perhaps St. Paul in Austin and its associated college the pinnacle of the state's Lutheran community. The young Socha assumed his new duties with enthusiasm, whereby the synod approved a $50 salary to direct Concordia's chorus and music appreciation instruction.[64] By this time, the chorus had expanded from its elite Octet to an ensemble of thirty men's voices, which "has made regular appearances at the church throughout the school year," a reference to their singing during regular worship services at St. Paul.[65] Under Socha's direction, the Treble Clef Choir of St. Paul was developed, singing its "first annual concert" in May 1945 and presenting "a variety of selections from the music of the church year," accompanied by guest organ soloist Elsie Lois Zabel, a University of Texas student who accompanied regularly at the church.[66] Socha's liturgical innovations included instituting a sung choral verset, offered by the mixed choir in September 1946, which rendered "the sentence for the Trinity season which will be given each Sunday henceforth till the Advent season."[67] For this same service, Socha could be found playing the music of Herzog and Heyser for prelude and postlude and Albert Beck's "Jesus' Little Lamb" as offertory,[68] Beck himself a composer, organist, and professor at Concordia, River Forest (1923–62), and possibly Socha's

---

64 "Docket of Business to Be Presented for Consultation with Dr. Paul Schulz, Chairman, Committee on Colleges," January 23, 1945 (University of North Texas Libraries, Portal to Texas History), https://texashistory.unt.edu/ark:/67531/metapth494524/ (accessed September 1, 2020).

65 "College Chorus to Sing Sunday at St. Paul," *Austin American* (May 5, 1945): 10.

66 "St. Paul Lutheran," *Austin American* (May 13, 1945): 28.

67 "Christian Home Series to Continue," *Austin American* (September 28, 1946): 2.

68 Ibid.

own teacher.[69] Socha continued his innovations in sacred music during Advent of that year when he instituted a formalized, fifteen-minute, preservice organ meditation on Advent themes for the evening services,[70] which the following Lent became a radio program of fifteen minutes on KVET featuring the choir performing music of the Lenten season.[71] Underscoring St. Paul's leadership in the LCMS community, Socha coordinated and directed a mass choir from five Lutheran churches in Austin in May 1947 to commemorate the centennial anniversary of the LCMS: "A mass choir of Austin Lutheran churches directed by John Socha, organist and choirmaster of St. Paul's Lutheran Church, will sing 'Beautiful Saviour' and the battle hymn of the Reformation, 'A Mighty Fortress is Our God' by Martin Luther. Lutheran clergymen will join the vested choir in procession from the courthouse to Wooldridge Park while singing 'Onward Christian Soldiers.' The same group will sing as the recessional hymn 'Now Thank We All Our God' set to music in 1648 by Johann Crueger."[72] Theatrics aside, one has to imagine the discomfort of several hundred "vested" choir members and clergy processing around Austin, singing Reformation hymns bedecked with a smattering of Victoriana provided by Sabine Baring-Gould's militant Sunday school song, all while sweltering under the blazing Texas sun!

The parish music ministry enhanced the Festival of Pentecost later that same month with a concert replacing the regular Sunday evening service:

---

69 "Beck, Albert," CCM, http://composers-classical-music.com/b/BeckAlbert .htm (accessed August 18, 2020).

70 "St. Paul's Offers Holy Communion," *Austin American* (December 7, 1946): 2.

71 "St. Paul Lutheran Church Presents the Choir of the Church," *Austin American* (March 1, 1947): 3.

72 "Lutheran Churches Join in Centennial Celebration," *Austin Statesman* (May 16, 1947): 1.

The evening service hour will be given over to a concert by the mixed choir of the church under John J. Socha's direction. After a semonette by the pastor of the church the choir will begin the musical theme: "Sacred Selections from the High Festivals of the Church Year." The concert will be introduced by the rendition of "A Mighty Fortress is Our God." The invocation will be sung in the chorale: "Lord Jesus Christ Be With Us Now." Advent and Christmas will be represented by numbers from Bach and Christiansen. The beautiful Lenton [sic] music of the Lutheran Church will be followed by the Easter hymn: "Christ the Lord is Risen Today." Mr. Socha will be at the organ for a special musical selection.[73]

Credit must be given to St. Paul's pastor, Rev. Albert Jesse, future president of the LCMS Texas District, for his discernment in encouraging such a program, which treacherously negotiated that line between worship and concert performance in which the music (and choir) is allowed to present the Word of God. This event was similar to a regular worship service, as it took place during the regularly scheduled worship time and was led by the pastor, who even delivered a sermonette. Yet the choir was allowed the rest of the service to catechize about the church year through sacred music. This event almost resembles an academic service such as the traditional Anglican Lessons and Carols, which is neither worship nor a concert but an academic service that bears discernable hallmarks of the former. Perhaps this expresses yet another connection between the parish and the nearby college in which a certain liturgical creativity and flexibility are permitted for the sake of catechesis. Socha's tenure at St. Paul was characterized by disciplined innovation and structured creativity that portended the liturgical renewal in the decades to come.

During Socha's tenure, St. Paul had been offered the opportunity to purchase land at Red River and East Thirty-Second

---

73 "St. Paul Plans Festival Rites," *Austin American* (May 24, 1947): 3.

Streets, immediately adjacent to Lutheran Concordia College, an opportunity the congregation quickly seized. Thus, in 1951, an auditorium-gymnasium had been completed, and an education building was finished in 1953, with each of the eight classrooms equipped with a "small, intricately carved altar, built and carved by Emil Schroeder."[74] A fine new church building constructed from Austin cut stone, hand cut and trimmed at the site, was completed in 1959, providing a sanctuary, chapel, administrative offices, choir room, and basement undercroft.[75] Although the old Hinners pipe organ was not suitable for the new church, which remained without a pipe organ for a few years, the lively acoustics of the new space certainly opened the ears of many in the congregation and the Austin community to the liturgical and musical possibilities.

The remainder of John Socha's career is far too interesting to omit from this account, although admittedly, it is characterized by less sacred music as the years proceed. After receiving a master's degree in education from the University of Texas, in 1951 he took a call to Pagedale, Missouri, to organize a consolidated Lutheran school while concurrently directing the Lutheran Hour Choir in St. Louis. Returning to Texas in 1957, he served as a principal, teacher, choir director, organist, and youth leader at Immanuel Lutheran in Giddings. Here he began his own newspaper column entitled "Horsin' Around by Mr. John," dedicated mostly to "horses and horse lovers."[76] He organized Western Weeks in Lee County, was a member of the Lee County Sheriff's Posse and president of the Giddings chamber of commerce, and lost his bid for Giddings mayor by five votes. Sensing a call to the ordained ministry, Socha graduated from Concordia Theological Seminary in Springfield, Illinois, in 1966, following which he was appointed to

74 "History of the First Fifty Years."
75 Ibid.
76 Holsomback, "He's a Pastor."

Figure 5.7 Rev. John Socha, a native of New Jersey but ultimately an enthusiastic Texan. (Source: Barbara Holsomback, "He's a Pastor for All Seasons," *Fort Worth Star-Telegram* [June 22, 1977]: 17.)

dual parishes in Sweeny and Freeport, Texas. Here he wrote a column about the local football team, as he recalled, "I wrote under the name of Mr. John . . . I would go to the football games every Saturday night. The games usually lasted until 10.30pm. I'd have my column called to the newspaper by midnight and then arrive home between 1–2am. Then I'd get up early Sunday and preach some of my best sermons."[77] In 1971, he accepted a call to Zion Lutheran in Fort Worth, where he was equally active in civic life. He retired to Giddings in 1980, returning to manage the chamber of commerce while still serving as the pastor of Trinity Lutheran in Dime Box. Having family connections in the Slovak Lutheran Church, he could speak his native language well and even navigate the Wendish language as spoken by the Lutherans in Lee County. He was a member of

---

77 Ibid.

the Texas Wendish Heritage Society and edited the organization's newsletter. He died on December 19, 1988.[78]

Postwar Development at Concordia College

During the first twelve years of the college's existence, enrollment hardly grew, with twenty-six students enrolled for the 1926–27 school year, in comparison to thirty-two students enrolled during the 1937–38 terms. The school had reached a high point in 1929–30, with fifty-eight students enrolled, but this counted as an outlier surrounded by more modest years.[79] The school had settled into a six-year course of study with a formalized boarding school for high school boys, capped by two years of normal school program study—in other words, the program that prepared young men for the teaching or ordained ministry. The Great Depression brought unexpected economic hardship to the school, with synodical budget cuts for higher education in 1932, during which salaries subsidized by the synod were cut 25 percent.[80] Yet the lean times would pass, whereby the academic year 1944 saw an enrollment of sixty-three, even though maximum capacity had been set at forty-one. By this time, the growth necessitated pleas to the synod for more storage room, additional buildings for extracurricular activities, an indoor physical education plant, a larger chapel,

---

78 George Smith, "John Socha, Musician and Educator," *Fort Worth Star Telegram* (December 21, 1988): 25.

79 "History of Lutheran Concordia College at Austin, Texas, 1926–1938," ca. 1938 (University of North Texas Libraries, Portal to Texas History), https://texashistory.unt.edu/ark:/67531/metapth606375/ (accessed September 2, 2020).

80 E. Seuel, letter to the Evangelical Lutheran Synod of Missouri Boards of Control, September 17, 1932 (University of North Texas Libraries, Portal to Texas History), https://texashistory.unt.edu/ark:/67531/metapth494517/ (accessed September 2, 2020).

and additional housing and kitchen space.[81] Indeed, increases in enrollment strained all the synodical colleges and seminaries, particularly at the end of the war with so many servicemen returning home ready to resume their educational careers. In 1946, the synod granted Concordia College $25,000 for expansion and renovation of the campus, which would result in the aforementioned significant improvements and modernizations over the next few years.[82]

The music curriculum, however, seemed to languish without clear direction, although that cannot be attributed to a lack of student interest. Minutes from the faculty meeting of October 15, 1942, indicate a recognition of the problem: "We need some new pianos. There are over 30 music students, they do not have enough time to practice."[83] The faculty's request to the synod for additional building funds included an imploration for suitable practice instruments to be placed in all "classrooms, living rooms, lounge room and chapel. If proper rooms were provided, we could get along with fewer instruments. There would be no playing during classes. Note [that] this bedlam is in a building where classes are taught—not only in the dormitory."[84] The mutually beneficial arrangement of prior decades with St. Paul to share music staff seems to have run its course. In fact, some rifts in the relationship between the parish and the college had begun to appear when, in 1946, the

---

81 "Docket of Business to Be Presented for Consultation with Dr. Paul Schulz, Chairman, Committee on Colleges," ca. 1944 (University of North Texas Libraries, Portal to Texas History), https://texashistory.unt.edu/ark:/67531/metapth494569/ (accessed September 2, 2020).

82 F. H. Stelzer, letter to George Beto, April 8, 1946 (University of North Texas Libraries, Portal to Texas History), https://texashistory.unt.edu/ark:/67531/metapth494636/ (accessed September 2, 2020).

83 "Lutheran Concordia College Faculty Meetings Minutes, 1930–1952," 1930–52 (University of North Texas Libraries, Portal to Texas History), https://texashistory.unt.edu/ark:/67531/metapth606265/ (accessed September 2, 2020): 21.

84 "Docket of Business," ca. 1944.

faculty recorded that Rev. Albert Jesse of St. Paul was "under the impression that he is the College Pastor and that St. Paul Church is the College Church. This matter is to be discussed with him at a future meeting of the faculty. It was stated that students have the right to visit other churches but that most of the students and the faculty attend services at St. Paul."[85] In recognition of the need for a more intentional music curriculum and activities, in April 1946, a Professor Huebschmann recruited twelve students for a new band.[86] John Socha, of course, directed the chorus, which apparently was relegated only to "one-half hour during the noon period," presumably weekly, and likewise taught music appreciation.[87] Already in 1945, while approving a semester's contract for Socha to teach, the synod had warned that "very few institutions are receiving any money for this purpose at this time, because in most cases this instruction is given by a regular professor. If, in time, something like this can be worked out at Austin, we prefer it."[88] Thus, dutifully, in 1946, the administration addressed the need for a more regular music teacher by appealing to River Forest, seeking a man with "at least two years of college, [who] should be able to teach music and perhaps Economics and Civics. We intend to pay the new man 100 dollars in addition to board and room for nine months."[89] This job description differed little from that of the professors in the early days of the Addison Teachers' Seminary, which required them to teach all manner of subjects, from classics to mathematics to music, although one is compelled to think that the instructors of the previous generations, steeped in the classical traditions of learning, knew more about the musical arts than those matriculating in more

85 "Lutheran Concordia College": 30.

86 Ibid.: 29.

87 Ibid.: 31.

88 "Docket of Business," January 23, 1945.

89 "Lutheran Concordia College": 33.

recent times. Nonetheless, although the administration's first choice of teacher declined the call, it was ultimately fulfilled by Carlos Messerli, then a student at River Forest. According to Messerli, "I taught piano, directed the choir (octet), [taught] economics and sociology, and assisted coaching basketball, in 1946–47. In 1947 I returned to Concordia Teachers College as a student in River Forest, IL."[90] He was also appointed as the organist of Grace Lutheran Church in Austin.[91] Messerli would lead a distinguished career as the professor of music at Concordia University, Seward, Nebraska, and as the founding director of the Lutheran Music Program.[92] One of Messerli's programs with the Octet, offered in 1947, explored the theme "Hymns of the Church Year," featuring congregational singing, organ solos, and an address on "The Lutheran Choral" by Professor George Beto.[93] This was no secular glee club performance but rather one that was centered on sacred music applied in its liturgical context, no doubt a positive formational experience for the young men preparing for careers in church work.

Yet temporary measures only provided temporary blessings. By late 1947, Professor Beto applied for permission

to secure the services of a competent music instructor. The comparatively large number of Normal [education] students in our student body and the fact that our entire music program is accredited by the State Department of Education and

90 Carlos Messerli, letter to archivist, n.d. (University of North Texas Libraries, Portal to Texas History), https://texashistory.unt.edu/ark:/67531/metapth494637/ (accessed September 2, 2020).

91 "Messerli Organist at Grace Church," *Austin American* (October 12, 1946): 2.

92 Carlos Messerli, *Thine the Amen* (Minneapolis: Lutheran University Press, 2005): 7.

93 "Hymns of the Christian Church Year," Concordia Lutheran College, Austin, TX, 1947 (University of North Texas Libraries, Portal to Texas History), https://texashistory.unt.edu/ark:/67531/metapth494548/ (accessed September 2, 2020).

the Southern Association forces us to offer a music program of some consequence.

For several years local music teachers, usually Christian Day School teachers, were hired on a part-time basis. They gave piano lessons to ministerial and non-ministerial as well as to Normal students. Synod paid the cost of the lessons of the Normal students and contributed $100–125 per year to cover the cost of giving choral instruction to the entire Student Body.

For obvious reasons this program of instruction was unsatisfactory. The music instruction was given at odd hours of the day, frequently during the recreational period. Since the music instructors were not members of the faculty, they often lacked the respect of the students, too, the local congregation did not look with favor on the plan because it involved its teachers in accepting "outside employment." There was a lack of uniformity in instruction. Each teacher stressed his or her "likes" in instructing the individual pupil.

For the past two years we have had either a River Forest or Seward vicar in charge of the music program. The vicar gave piano lessons to all students desiring such instruction. Synod was charged one dollar per lesson for each Normal student; the parents of any other students taking piano lessons were charged an equal sum. The vicar also supervised choral instruction and taught one subject. . . . While the plan has been a marked improvement over the previous program of music instruction, it does not approximate the ideal. Since we are forced to change teachers each year, the program lacks continuity. Music teachers tell us that this frequent change of teachers is a cardinal defect in our program. Too, vicars lack sufficient maturity.[94]

Indeed, this manner of instruction belies the method employed by the early synodical schools, which stressed music by funding a full-time professor, even when resources were limited. Now

---

94 George Beto, letter to Martin Neeb, December 12, 1947 (University of North Texas Libraries, Portal to Texas History), https://texashistory.unt .edu/ark:/67531/metapth494645/ (accessed September 2, 2020).

amid relative abundance, the political will to hire a competent music professor seemed beyond the ability of Concordia's board of control. Perhaps maintaining quality music instruction for its students was easier to do at River Forest, which already had eighty years of proven success to buttress support for a music program as an integral part of its teaching curriculum. Recalling the words of J. W. Behnken, this does perhaps exemplify the complicated reality that Texas was still a pioneer frontier, in which music was simply an adjunct luxury.

Several years would have to pass before a professional musician could be funded, likely to the detriment of the student body, who occasionally sought to participate in the local parish choirs, which the faculty discouraged unless they chose to walk to St. Paul.[95] In the meantime, the school continued with music as best it could. Professor Bernard Kurweg directed the twenty-one voices of the Concordia Choristers in 1949 on Christmas and spring tours throughout Texas.[96] A Hammond organ was purchased in late 1949.[97] The school adopted a junior college model in 1951, made possible by the campus building projects (including dormitories, a chapel, and a dining hall) that had been completed or were in progress with synod funding.[98] Thus, the college would continue its rapid growth and development during the latter half of the twentieth century.

---

95 "Lutheran Concordia College": 32.
96 "Concordia College Class of '49," Concordia Lutheran College, Austin, TX, 1949 (University of North Texas Libraries, Portal to Texas History), https://texashistory.unt.edu/ark:/67531/metapth494540/ (accessed September 2, 2020): 21.
97 "Lutheran Concordia College": 30.
98 Ibid.: 40.

6

A New Direction for Advanced Sacred Music Studies in Texas

In August 1952, Ivan Ronald Olson began his duties as the instructor of music at Concordia, the first full-time appointment of a music faculty in the school's history, representing a significant investment in music.[1] Olson's hiring represented a final break between the music programs of the college and St. Paul parish, as the college now declared its independence through hiring someone not associated with the church. Olson, born in Soldier, Iowa, in 1928, had graduated from the University of Iowa in 1950 with a BA and was a newly minted 1952 graduate of the University of Texas, having studied piano with Dalies Frantz, a student of Schnabel and Horowitz and an occasional movie actor.[2] Olson had taught public school music in Austin[3] and would take over choral duties at Concordia. Also breaking with tradition, Olson served as the organist at

---

1 "Lutheran Concordia College Faculty Meetings Minutes, 1930–1952," 1930–52 (University of North Texas Libraries, Portal to Texas History), https://texashistory.unt.edu/ark:/67531/metapth606265/ (accessed September 2, 2020): 2.

2 "Recital Set at Concordia Tuesday at 8," *Austin American* (April 24, 1955): 57; Kate Rudolph, "Dalies Frantz: Denver's Titan of the Keyboard," Denver Library, August 25, 2014, https://history.denverlibrary.org/news/dalies-frantz-denvers-titan-keyboard (accessed August 17, 2020).

3 "Concordia Begins Year September 1," *Austin American* (August 26, 1952): 28.

First Lutheran Church in Austin, a non-LCMS congregation.[4]
Although Olson lacked synodical credentials, he apparently
had garnered the trust of the faculty, as evidenced in a curious
incident only two months into his tenure, in October 1952, as
reported in the faculty meeting minutes:

> As a first item of report President Beto indicated that one of
> the pastors in the local conference had raised the question
> about the use of the negro spiritual in the repertoire of the
> Concordia Choristers. There was limited discussion arising
> from the announcement. Finally Mr. Olson mentioned that he
> was attempting to create variety and to fit to a degree the taste
> of the Choristers in the selection of music. The faculty deter-
> mined by general consent to place confidence in Mr. Olson
> as a qualified director of the singing group. If no sacrilege is
> involved in the text of a selection and if there is no intent to
> elicit ridicule, there can be no valid objection to the choice of
> sacred music for the Choristers' use.[5]

Olson brought a new repertoire in general to the chorus, unencumbered as he was by LCMS tradition and the composers
and teachers at Addison or River Forest, who heretofore had
been such a significant influence in the music of the candidates
who served in Austin. His first Christmas concert, held in the
school's badly needed new gymnasium, featured traditional
Bach chorales ("How Bright Appears the Morning Star" and
"Break Forth, O Beauteous Heavenly Light") in addition to
"Carol of the Bells," other traditional carols, and the previously
maligned spirituals "Mary Had a Baby" and "Go Tell It on the
Mountain."[6] Olson again displayed his penchant for nontradi-
tional programming when in May 1954 he prepared the

---

4 "Danna Foster, Ivan Olson, United in Lutheran Church," *American
    Statesman* (July 15, 1956): 14.
5 "Lutheran Concordia College": 8.
6 "Concordia Presenting Song Festival," *Austin Statesman* (December 17,
    1952): 20.

medieval morality play *Everyman* as a "dramatic vehicle selected as the presentation of the junior class," to which the choristers contributed choral settings, "settings of the De Profundis, the Te Deum, and sections of the ancient church Propers."[7] The new memorial gymnasium provided a much-needed performance space for this venture in *Gesamtkunstwerk* and would also host solo performances, as when Olson played a piano recital of Haydn ("Andante con Variazioni in F Minor"), Bach ("Toccata in D Major"), Beethoven ("32 Variations on an Original Theme in C-Minor"), Prokofiev ("Visions Fugitives"), and Chopin ("Ballade no. IV in F-Minor") in 1955. Growth in the music program necessitated hiring organist Ronald Trampe as an instructor in music.[8] Trampe would serve as an accompanist for Olson's increasingly ambitious programs.

Olson deployed his musical resources with creativity. Those boys enrolled in the high school component of the school received no formal music classes but were able to participate in their own four-part baritone (TTBB) chorus. Olson directed a "Festival of Song" in May 1955, presented by the college-age Choristers and the high school choir. An eclectic affair of six sections, highlights included secular "college and novelty" songs and the introduction of the Concords, a "campus rhythm and blues quartet," while the high school boys sang patriotic music and the Choristers sang more spirituals, all concluding with Randall Thompson's "The Testament of Freedom."[9] The introduction of coeducation at the college level in the autumn of 1955 provided new opportunities for music, and the mixed Chapel Choir was formed to "sing at daily chapel services and to present daily chapel services and to present programs in

---

7 "Concordia College Sets Plays Wednesday Night," *Austin American* (May 19, 1954): 12.
8 "Rev. Zeeb to Be Feted," *Austin American* (September 23, 1955): 15.
9 "Song Festival Planned at Concordia Friday," *Austin Statesman* (May 2, 1955): 9.

Figure 6.1 Ivan Olson.
(Source: "Concordia Choir
to Give Program Here,"
Fort Worth Star-Telegram
[February 26, 1964]: 13.)

church of the surrounding area,"[10] also providing an opportunity for Olson to explore new choral literature.[11] By 1957, the
Chapel Choir had grown to thirty-five mixed voices, offering
sufficient forces for Olson to program Richard Wienhorst's
The Seven Words of Christ from the Cross,[12] a recent (1954)
work from the Valparaiso University composer,[13] during their

---

10 "Concordia's Chapel Choir Sings Sunday," *Austin American* (May 1,
   1959): 19.
11 "Students Guests of Kiwanis Club," *Austin Statesman* (November 8,
   1955): 14.
12 "Concordia Choir Will Sing Friday at Zion Church," *Fort Worth Star
   Telegram* (March 11, 1957): 11.
13 "Richard William Wienhorst," fold3.com, https://www.fold3.com/
   memorial/111664892/richard-william-wienhorst (accessed January 22,
   2022).

annual spring tour. Continuing his proclivity for contemporary works and highlighting his female singers, Olson programmed Benjamin Britten's *Ceremony of Carols* for women's voices for an Advent/Christmas program in December 1959 at St. Paul, bringing in Joel Andrews, professor of harp at the University of Texas, to accompany.[14] For the Christmas program of 1963, Olson's ensembles performed Vaughan Williams's "Fantasia on Christmas Carols"; Buxtehude's cantata on "Wachet Auf," accompanied by two violins, cello, and harpsichord; as well as anthems by Britten, Kodály, and the requisite spirituals. Ronald Trampe played organ, while a new instructor of music, Dorothy Meyer, accompanied the Buxtehude cantata on the harpsichord. The instrumentation employed here is of interest, as it represents the first time on record that a musical performance at Concordia had attempted to consider historical performance practice concerns in its accompanimental forces.[15]

The completion of Birkmann Chapel in 1952 provided the college with space for corporate worship. Although modest in size, the chapel sported an even more modest choir loft, which at least offered the semblance of reserved choral space. The college commissioned a new organ from the Reuter Organ Company of Lawrence, Kansas, in 1958, which was ready for dedication in 1959. Designed by Reuter in collaboration with Olson and Trampe, the organ

> contains eight ranks of pipes, most of which are free standing and exposed to view. Provisions were made in the organ for the addition of more ranks in the near future.
>
> Low wind pressures, un-nicked voicing, and adroit use of flute type sounds give the organ the brilliance and charm

---

14 "Ceremony of Carols Set Sunday," *Austin American* (December 11, 1959): 43.

15 "Concordia Christmas Music Rings Friday," *Austin American* (December 8, 1963): 26.

sought by German and Dutch builders of several centuries past.[16]

Romanticized newspaper accounts aside, Reuter's op. 1287 was an unexceptional instrument. Lacking reeds, its eight ranks were hindered by the chapel's low ceiling and dry acoustics, which reinforced its lack of color. Nonetheless, it represented the school's first real organ that could be used for teaching, practice, performance, and leading liturgical music, an important advancement for the school and a tangible benefit for organ students.

By this time, Olson had begun doctoral studies in sacred music at Union Theological Seminary in New York City,[17] studying composition with Alec Wyton and deputizing for him at the Cathedral of St. John the Divine. His cantata on "Christ lag in Todesbanden" (1961) was a project for Union. The cantata, "arranged for baritone, soprano, choir and organ," formed the centerpiece for a concert by the Concordia choirs in April 1961.[18] Graduating with his doctorate in 1964, Olson departed Concordia at the end of the spring semester to teach at American River College in Sacramento, where his roles over the next twenty-eight years would include professor of music and chairman and interim dean of the College of Fine Arts and where he would initiate an organ program. At his death in 2009, one colleague recalled him as "an incredible professor. . . . He was very knowledgeable about repertoire and loved 20th-century music. He was always interested in new composers." Another remembered that "he was not afraid to tackle lengthy, challenging

---

16 "Dedication Set for New Organ," *Austin Statesman* (January 7, 1960): 20. The organ was never expanded. One of the windchests (of four ranks) was purchased by Lord of Life Lutheran Church in Plano, Texas, in 2008, when this author was the director of music there, to create an antiphonal choir division.

17 "Concordia's Chapel Choir": 19.

18 "Concordia Choir Sets Program," *Austin American* (April 30, 1961): 23.

Figure 6.2 Birkmann Chapel in 1959. (Source: Birkmann Chapel, 1959 [University of North Texas Libraries, Portal to Texas History], https://texashistory.unt.edu/ark:/67531/metapth20192/ [accessed February 2, 2022].)

works."[19] One can discern even from his early career his propensity for modern, even challenging, choral music, and certainly, his interests guided the Concordia music program to perform contemporary music with attention to detail and performance practice. The growth of Concordia, particularly from its coeducational integration, found Olson at the school at a mutually opportune time, as much of the repertoire he had grown to prefer would have been impossible to perform with only male voices.

The trajectory of the music program at Concordia, which would form the aesthetic preferences of so many of the eventual pastors, teachers, and increasingly, laypeople who would graduate from the school, certainly now aimed in a different direction than, say, the seminary in Addison had envisioned in

---

19 "Ivan Olson, 81, Organist, Innovative ARC Teacher," *Sacramento Bee* (June 23, 2009): B6.

the nineteenth century for its teachers, for all of whom organ/ keyboard/singing study was a requirement, and concerted choral works of any complexity, much less rendered with any faithfulness to current performance practice standards, were eschewed. Concordia in Austin had never really modeled its musical educational component after Addison anyway, its lack of organ study requirement only one example. In 1954, as the faculty pondered a four-semester curriculum for the new junior college, only one class of unspecified "music," of two credit hours in the first semester, was required, the same as physical education. Even as musical opportunities for the students grew with a new band and multiple choruses with manifold performance opportunities each year, these were increasingly relegated to extracurricular activities, arguably less important than sports. This is not necessarily as condemnatory as it sounds, as this has been the direction of university studies in the United States at the time, and even into the twenty-first century. The specialization required for many professions now necessarily mitigates against a broad, classical education, and most Lutheran schools no longer expect their teachers to play organ. The congregations have changed and ideas about vocation have changed, and that is not necessarily for the worse. After all, the requirement that every teacher learn to play the organ certainly resulted in producing many reluctant organists whose lack of interest in music served neither their congregation nor the church music they were meant to enliven. For every teacher who discovered a love of organ and sacred music, how many only approached it as a chore? Rather, this narrative may instead elucidate how increasingly less integrated sacred music had become to the college experience of teaching and preministerial students as the twentieth century progressed. As most Concordia graduates would stay in Texas, their musical experiences at the college would find expression at their local parishes.

A New Professor, a New Perspective

Harold (Hal) Rutz, arriving as the professor of music and chair of the Fine Arts Department in the autumn of 1964, lacked no synodical credentials. A Milwaukee native, he began early piano study with Gerhard Schroth, the founding director of the Walther League Acappella Choir (now the Lutheran Acappella Choir of Milwaukee)[20] and the director of music at Mt. Olive Lutheran, switching to organ at age twelve, a student of Hugo Gehrke at Immanuel Lutheran. Rutz attended all six years of high school and junior college at Concordia, Milwaukee, where he sang in the choir under Harold Albers as well as in Schroth's a cappella chorus. Completing his sophomore year at Milwaukee, he transferred as a junior to Concordia, River Forest, where he studied organ with Carl Halter and Paul Bunjes. Zion Lutheran Church in Detroit issued him a call in 1952 to serve as a teacher and musician. Under the leadership of Rev. Kenneth Runge, the congregation tended toward High Church, even offering saints' days masses, which the entire parochial school would attend. Rutz taught fifth and sixth grades while managing to direct an adult and small children's choir, the growth of which was hindered by Zion's location in the inner city. He accepted a call in 1956 to Immanuel Lutheran in Kansas City, seeing the potential for a larger music program. The congregation already had a fine parish choir, a school of three hundred students, a high school girls' choir, and three school choirs, of which he directed one, all while teaching sixth grade and playing organ. During the summers, he studied for his master's degree in church music at Northwestern University, concurrently studying organ at nearby St. Luke's Episcopal Church with Thomas Matthews. For his graduate recital at Northwestern at St. Luke's Church in July 1960, Rutz performed Hanff's

---

20 See the Lutheran Acappella Choir of Milwaukee home page: https://www.lutheranacappella.org/the-choir.html.

"Ein feste Burg"; Bach's Prelude and Fugue in E-Minor ("The Wedge"), BWV 548; Franck's "Prelude, Fugue, and Variation," op. 18; Flor Peeters's "Modale Suite," op. 43; Langlais's "Prelude Modal," no. 1 of the *24 Pieces*; and Hindemith's entire Sonata no. 1 for Organ.[21] At Immanuel in Kansas City, Rutz enjoyed mentoring the student teachers from Concordia Teachers College in Seward, Nebraska, who were regularly posted to the school. These positive experiences with the student teachers, and his desire to focus on music exclusively in his career, happily compelled him to accept the call to teach at Concordia, Austin, in 1964.

Rutz's arrival coincided with the gradual elimination of the high school, which was phasing out. It offered only preministerial studies to boys, with Latin, Greek, Bible, and theology forming the core curriculum, and had no music classes other than an extracurricular choir. Concordia Lutheran College, "once an institution devoted exclusively to educating Lutheran church workers . . . changed its aims and aspirations in 1966 in keeping with the changing needs of the students it serves . . . announcing plans to expand the school to serve Austin as a two-year liberal arts college while maintaining its role in educating Lutherans to become ministers, teachers and other church workers."[22] By the end of the 1960s, the twenty-acre campus boasted three dormitories and a new science building as well as the dining hall, chapel, library, and its existing academic buildings. Two hundred students studied "data processing, introduction to computers, business mathematics, bookkeeping, business law, and personnel management" as well as "police administration, insurance fundamentals, and

21 "Northwestern University School of Music Student Recital: Harold Rutz," July 10, 1960, personal archive of Harold Rutz.
22 "Concordia Offers Personal Teaching," *Austin American* (February 28, 1969): 57.

mathematics of electronics."[23] The school was still a locus for educating Lutheran teachers, but its president at the time, Milton Riemer, nurtured expansive visions for Concordia to serve as a junior college for the entire region, acknowledging that the "big problem is persuading the citizens of Austin that we have a good school."[24] Although the school still offered training for Lutheran teachers, it had become much more than that.

Rutz directed the high school TTBB choir until it was discontinued in 1966, plumbing the depths of the repertoire to find suitable music, occasionally taking the choir to sing at a local church but offering no formal concerts. The junior college mixed choir, which was occasionally supplemented by the high school boys during the first two years, sang only sacred music, relying on the offerings of Concordia Publishing House (CPH) and Augsburg to supply traditional Lutheran repertoire, some by contemporary arrangers. This mixed choir was supplemented with a women's chorus directed by Dorothy Meyer Zielke. The junior choir would continue its spring tour tradition, and the choirs would perform a Christmas concert in the sumptuous acoustics of neighboring St. Paul, which by this time merely provided a performance space, as elegant as it now was. Rutz taught two semesters of music theory and two semesters of music history, plus keyboard, which thus constituted the entire music curriculum. Interestingly, all education students had to study keyboard, but nonmajors or preseminary students were exempt. Perhaps this reflected the actual practice for many years, in which the administration had lamented their lack of pianos, lack of practice space, and inconsistency of pedagogy, implying the demand for keyboard training was always high, if not particularly formalized, in the curriculum. Keyboard study was now a part of the curriculum for parish

23 "Concordia College's Growth in Recent Years Detailed," *Austin American* (August 14, 1969): 83.
24 Ibid.

education majors, as it had been elsewhere for decades. Rutz utilized a small piano lab of maybe six instruments and was assisted by Ronald Trampe in what must have been a bustling hive of activity, considering the students' practice needs too. Rutz taught an organ studio of seven to eight students each semester, utilizing the Reuter organ of the chapel.

A Texan Organ for the Mother Church of the LCMS in Austin

St. Paul in Austin extended a divine call to Bernard Gastler, a 1953 graduate of Concordia Teachers College in Seward, Nebraska, to teach and assume parish music duties in 1963.[25] Rev. Albert Jesse must have anticipated the wariness any trained musician would have accepting a call to a church with only a Hammond organ, writing to Gastler in his call documents, "Plans are underway to obtain a pipe organ to cost not more than $25,000. . . . The absolute deadline for the installation of the new organ would be the 75th anniversary of the church."[26] Since 1951, the church had been in discussions with organ builders, and a loft suitable for a pipe organ had intentionally been included in the church designs. In 1964, the church executed a contract with Otto Hofmann for a forty-three-rank organ at a cost of $28,460. Hofmann was an important local organ builder, and the instrument at St. Paul was one his most significant and certainly most successful.[27]

Otto Jürgen Hofmann was born in Kyle, Texas, in 1918, raised a Baptist. After studying acoustics and physics at the University of Texas, after World War II, his focus turned to

---

25 "Founder," Austin Children's Choir, https://austinchildrenschoir.org/ about/founder/ (accessed September 2, 2020).
26 From Gastler's informal recollections on a typed document from Harold Rutz.
27 Ibid.

Figure 6.3 St. Paul Lutheran Church, Austin, was constructed of native Texas limestone. (Source: Courtesy of Jeremy Clifton.)

organ building. Having traveled throughout Europe to hear historic instruments, his early influences were those continental builders who held most faithfully to eighteenth-century building techniques. Hofmann early appropriated the cause of the *Orgelbewegung*, or "Organ Reform Movement," espousing low wind pressures; clean, "singing" voicing techniques; mechanical action when possible; and a specification that provided color through differences in pitch rather than a reliance on foundation tone.[28] In the words of David Polley, former organist at St. Paul, "Hofmann stands at the center of a circle of Texas organ builders who continue and expand the concepts he first articulated in the 1950s."[29] Through the years, thousands of Concordia students would experience its leadership of the

28 Benjamin A. Kolodziej, "A History of Pipe Organs in the Lone Star State," *The Tracker*, Vol. 63, No. 3 (July 2019): 15–23.

29 David J. Polley, "Otto Hofmann: Texas Organbuilder (1950–1967)," 1993 (ETD collection of the University of Nebraska–Lincoln), https://digitalcommons.unl.edu/dissertations/AAI9415940 (accessed January 22,

liturgy and Lutheran hymnody, and hundreds of organ students would study, accompany, perform, or play a service or
recital on the instrument, not to mention the hundreds of students in the parish school for whom it would constitute a part
of their spiritual life.

Hofmann himself wrote in the dedication program, antici-
pating the importance of the instrument:

> Not often do we have the opportunity to build an organ where
> there is a good church building, a strong congregation, and a
> wonderful Lutheran musical heritage, and also have the confi-
> dence of knowing of the high quality of the music that will be
> played on this instrument.
>
> With this happy combination we endeavored to build an
> especially Lutheran organ reflecting such typically Lutheran
> characteristics as strength, assurance, firmness in one's belief,
> compassion, and Christian joy which pours forth in song.
>
> With special emphasis on hymn singing in the church, the
> tonal design of the organ was conceived to bring again con-
> gregational hymn singing to that peak which once made the
> Lutheran worship service unique in the history of the world's
> religious . . . music.[30]

Incumbent organist Bernard Gastler enthusiastically logged
organ progress during the spring of 1967 in a written journal, happily recording "First sounds of installed set of pipes!"
or conversely lamenting "Organ builders did not work this
week at all!" Nonetheless, the organ was finished enough for
a short dedication service the morning of May 28, 1967, Bach's
"Ein feste Burg" the first official piece to be played on the new
organ, of which Gastler recalls in the third person, "Thrill-
ing experience for organist."[31] The main service at 11:00 a.m.

2022): 6. This dissertation is the definitive reference for Hofmann's life
and career.

30 From the personal files of Hal Rutz.

31 From Gastler's informal recollections in the collection of Hal Rutz.

was televised, with over nine hundred people in attendance. The organ was used for Concordia's baccalaureate service at 4:30 p.m. that day. Paul Rosel of Concordia Teachers College in Seward, Nebraska, played the dedication recital on July 16, 1967, although curiously, the reed pipes did not arrive until the next month. Hal Rutz performed the second dedication recital in August, playing the music of J. S. Bach, Pasquini, Krebs, and others,[32] in conjunction with a Texas District Lutheran Teachers' Conference, in which "many Lutheran teachers were quite interested in hearing the organ."[33] At the time, Rutz lauded the instrument as producing "the clear, precise and brilliant tone characteristic of Northern European organs in Germany and Denmark."[34] In a program designed to feature this organ's novel baroque sounds, Dr. Frank Speller of the University of Texas performed an all-Bach recital in May 1969.[35]

Sacred Music Pedagogy Evolves at Concordia

Throughout most of the 1970s, the music curriculum remained largely unchanged. The two primary choirs, the Chapel Choir and the College Choir, continued to rehearse and perform under Rutz's direction, highlights of the year being the annual Advent or Christmas program at St. Paul and the annual spring tour. Programs from this decade reveal the choir learning music by leading contemporary Lutheran composers such as Paul Manz, Charles Ore, Paul Bunjes, Paul Christiansen, and Jan Bender; non-Lutheran living composers such as Natalie Sleeth and Donald Marsh; as well as standard choral repertoire from Bach, Cornelius, Buxtehude, Billings, and Holst, Scheidt,

---

32 "Organ Recital," *Austin Statesman* (August 10, 1967): 37.
33 Hal Rutz, personal correspondence with the author, August 2020.
34 "Concordia Choir to Sing Religious Program Tonight," *Austin American* (April 24, 1969): 52.
35 "Organ Professor to Present Recital," *Austin American* (May 9, 1969): 36.

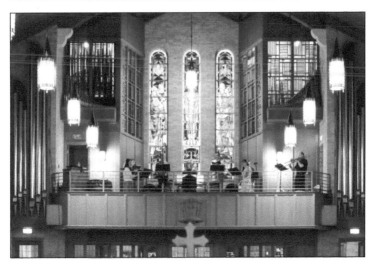

Figure 6.4 The 1967 Hofmann organ at St. Paul. (Source: Courtesy of Jeremy Clifton.)

among others, providing not only a great variety of music for the audience but also a diversity of programming for the students to experience. Rutz always intentionally programmed Bach's music, and his philosophy for tour programs was to present interesting, winsome music rather than the avant-garde, but still not necessarily what the average church choirs were singing.

At his ten-year anniversary at Concordia, Rutz became eligible for a one-semester sabbatical, which he took in the autumn of 1975, his family in tow, spending time at Cambridge University, participating in lectures, and studying organ with Peter Hurford at St. Alban's Cathedral.[36] He attended the Interna-

---

36 These biweekly lessons were held at Hurford's home. Hurford chose carefully the repertoire each student would study, with Rutz remembering at least one Bach trio sonata assigned to him. About ten students participated in this rather informal study program, which concluded with a studio recital at St. Alban's Cathedral, for which there was no rehearsal time and for which Hurford himself registered each piece.

tional Organ Festival at St. Alban's and studied for a month in Vienna with Michael Radulescu at the Summer Mastercourse for Organists.[37] Rutz remembers returning to Austin enriched by this experience. He returned to Cambridge for a similarly structured sabbatical ten years later.

By the late 1970s, under the leadership of president Dr. Ray F. Martens, Concordia was entertaining the notion of expanding to a four-year college, initiating a $3 million campaign for building renovations and new facilities in the spring of 1980, adding a year to the college with each subsequent class until 1982, at which time the first class graduated from the new four-year institution, the fourth such college in Austin, with mayor Carole Keeton McClellan predicting "that the college will play a large role in Austin's growth."[38] Hal Rutz remembers spending the preceding two years expanding the music curriculum to accommodate courses leading to a new bachelor's degree in parish music, which would be offered with an organ or conducting concentration, the overall curriculum modeled after the programs offered by the Concordias at River Forest and Seward. Rutz continued to teach seven to eight organ students each year, the majority of which were parish education majors. Graduates of the parish music major, like those of the education major, would receive divine calls administered on the synodical level. Although parish music graduates were increasingly finding placement in the state, Rutz recalled that there were not many full-time teacher/musician positions in the Texas District.

In 1982, Bernard Gastler was appointed as the professor of music at Concordia, although he would maintain his connection at St. Paul. Under his own initiative and with Concordia's support, Gastler founded the Austin Children's Choir in 1986,

---

37 "Concordia's Chapel Choir": 19.
38 "Concordia Seeks Funds," *Austin American-Statesman* (April 10, 1980): 19.

Figure 6.5 Dr. Bernard (Bernie) Gastler. (Source: Courtesy of the Gastler family.)

inspired after a trip to England left him with "the sound of boy choirs in his ear."[39] Also in 1982, the college purchased a two-manual, three-rank Klug and Schumacher mechanical-action practice organ.

Louise T. Peter, a granddaughter of Jan Kilian, donated $4 million for a new fine arts center on the Concordia campus, which was dedicated in 1987.[40] The Peter Center would house music practice rooms, faculty offices, gallery space, a TV studio, and Schroeder Auditorium, a concert hall that had been worked into the architectural plans at Rutz's urging. He knew the university needed an organ of concert quality, and he likewise knew this would be the only building that could house it. At his insistence, the plans for the auditorium had included a stage that Rutz was certain would be able to fit an organ. The

39　Randy Harriman, "Shostakovich for the Younger Set," *Austin American-Statesman* (November 5, 2006): 105.

40　Grace Lim, "Concordia Dedicates TV Center," *Austin American-Statesman* (September 20, 1987): 20.

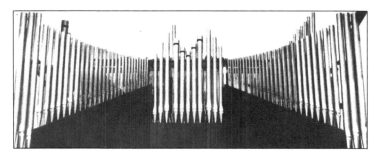

Figure 6.6 The reconfigured Schlicker organ in the Louise T. Peter Center. (Source: Courtesy of Hal Rutz.)

opportunity to install an organ would come only late in the construction process. St. John's College in Winfield, Kansas, a two-year college of the LCMS founded in 1893, had closed in 1986, and its 1960 Schlicker chapel organ was offered for sale. Seizing the opportunity, Rutz secured the organ for purchase by Concordia, only to find that the stage that had been carefully designed for an organ was just shy of the dimensions required to house the organ. Nonetheless, as the building was still under construction, the architects were able to revise their plans for the north wall in order for a steel cantilever to be constructed. Rutz remembers that had the opportunity to purchase the Schlicker come only six months later, the building process would have been too far along, and the instrument could not have been accommodated.

Thus, on a Sunday afternoon in January 1988, Hal Rutz dedicated the two-manual, thirty-three-rank Schlicker organ in Schroeder Auditorium. The instrument had been designed by Dr. Paul Bunjes of Concordia in River Forest, and as such, the two-manual specification was not without its eccentricities—most notably, the inclusion of a 2 Schalmei on the pedal. The auditorium's acoustics were never particularly hospitable. Nonetheless, the organ was able to perform much concert literature and provided a more suitable teaching instrument than the limited

Reuter in the chapel. The organ was the focus of many summer church music workshops initiated by Rutz in the 1980s after the completion of the Peter Center. Rutz brought acclaimed clinicians and organists to teach and lecture for sometimes as many as 150 church musicians from Texas and surrounding states. Donald Busarow, David Cherwien, Michael Burkhardt, John Folkening, and Carl Schalk were only a few of the lecturers who taught during these workshops, which also allowed fellowship and networking among Texan church musicians. Throughout his career, Rutz himself maintained a prominent role in Texas Lutheran musician circles, routinely performing organ recitals around the state, a few of his organ dedications including Our Redeemer Lutheran in Dallas (1969), Memorial Lutheran in Houston (1972), Redeemer Lutheran in Odessa (1974), Trinity Lutheran in Tyler (1974), and Shepherd of the Hills in San Antonio (1976).[41]

A new pipe organ in classical style built by the Houston firm Visser-Rowland replaced the old Reuter in Birkmann Chapel in the mid-1990s. Hal Rutz retired in 1996 after a career of three decades at Concordia, guiding many Lutheran teachers and parish musicians in their musical studies. Faythe Freese, a recitalist and teacher, replaced Rutz as the music professor. After she left for the University of Alabama, Dr. Jonathan Eifert served as music professor until the school, now a university, moved to a new campus in 2008, at which time the historic campus was demolished. Meanwhile, Kathleen Achterberg faithfully served as the director of music for many years at St. Paul Lutheran Church, her husband, Robert, having spent much of his career directing the instrumental music program at Concordia.

Lutheran Concordia College was conceived by the people of St. Paul Lutheran out of a desire to provide a Lutheran education to Texas boys and to college-age youth preparing for either

---

41 Programs from the personal files of Hal Rutz.

the ordained or teaching ministries. Unlike its predecessor schools in Illinois or Nebraska, the study of sacred music was less integrated into the overall curriculum, particularly in the early years. It is difficult to indict that early leadership for this, as Texas was still somewhat of a frontier. As Jan Kilian had experienced in the 1860s and 1870s, Lutherans in Texas could too easily be isolated from the rest of the country, necessarily fostering a sense of independence, individualism, or even distrust. Resources, from books to organs to pianos, were hard to obtain in the early years, a problem alleviated only by the expansion of railroads. The climate during the summer could be stiflingly humid while obstinately muddy at other seasons. Further, the Lutherans in Texas came from diverse groups. The Wendish differed in their culture and liturgical practices from the Germans, who themselves could range from Low Church semi-Methodists who preferred conventicles to those of more High Church inclinations. These differences were only enhanced by the vast geography of the state, which precluded easy travel and social interactions. Still, the college had always maintained some form of sacred music instruction, whether on an adjunct basis, borrowing the expertise of those musicians at St. Paul, or through full-time professionals as would be hired from the 1950s on. Luther's observation that music is "next" to the Word of God in its importance, although manifest differently in this Austin school than elsewhere, was still exemplified in the many years of faithful music teaching, sacred concerts, and musically oriented liturgies of utmost creativity and beauty.

7

The Developing Vocation of the Church Musician

When Richard Resch was ordained into the office of the holy ministry in 1988 at Concordia Theological Seminary in Fort Wayne, he was bestowed the title of "Kantor," the first usage of that term in the LCMS in the modern day. Although he had been a contract musician at the seminary since 1977, his vocation would now expand beyond that of organist, choirmaster, and musical administrator, his musical skills now infused with theological acumen and pastoral awareness,[1] hearkening back to Johann Walter (1496–1570), Luther's musician, whose assistance in preparing the *Deutsche Messe* of 1526 was informed as much by theological aptitude as by musical proficiency. The usage of *Kantor* suggests much more than an ascription of utilitarian, post-Enlightenment enumeration of job duties, as Paul Westermeyer explains: "In the German Lutheran tradition the cantor was in charge of music for the congregation, music and musical instruction in the school, and music for the city. He was responsible for the people's singing of the liturgy and hymns; directed the *Kantorei* and deployed its vocal and instrumental forces as needed in church, school, and city, and composed *Gebrauchsmusik*—occasional music—for weddings, funerals,

---

1 Rev. Richard Resch, personal correspondence with the author, September 25, 2020.

and civic functions along with pieces for services throughout the church year, such as cantatas. Johann Walter, Johann
Eccard, Johann Crüger, and J. S. Bach were all cantors."[2]
The Kantor's vocation was intimately interwoven with the
people to whom he ministered, his musical skills often secondary to pastoral abilities. Herbert Neuchterlein expounds upon
the necessity of the Kantor's proper spiritual background, here
specifically in reference to J. S. Bach's application for the Thom-
askirche vacancy:

> A cantor hoping to secure a job needed more than teach-
> ing ability and specific musical qualifications. He was also
> required to commit himself to a certain doctrinal position. . . .
> Because of his dual role in the school and the church, the Ger-
> man cantor provided an important liaison between the clergy
> and the teaching staff. He carried full responsibility for the
> school music program, and he was the minister of sacred
> music in the life of the congregation. . . .
>   For all of this, the Lutheran cantor viewed the use of his
> artistic gifts primarily as a summons from God to preach the
> Gospel. He did not consider himself an individual artist who
> was to receive honor and acclaim through his own doing. He
> regarded his work as existing only for the reason of purpose-
> ful union with God and the church.[3]

The Kantor's position, then, required musical training, theological education, significant teaching responsibilities, direction
of the music in the parish community, and humble submission
as a servant of Word and Sacrament. Although Richard Resch's
ordination may have precipitated the modern renewal of the term
Kantor, ordination has never been a requirement for the proper

---

2 Paul Westermeyer, *The Church Musician* (Minneapolis: Augsburg Fortress, 1997): 15.
3 Herbert Neuchterlein, "Cantor," in *Key Words in Church Music: Definition Essays on Concepts, Practices, and Movements of Thought in Church
  Music*, ed. Carl Schalk (St. Louis, MO: CPH, 1978): 45.

exercise of this musical vocation, nor has precedent ever suggested that a Kantor can only find full vocational fulfillment in ordination. Most Kantors in the LCMS, whether utilizing that title or one of the more utilitarian descriptors, have generally been laypeople. Using the appellation *Kantor* here is less important than the vocation implied.

Tracing the Kantorate in Texas

The history of the sacred music profession in the United States in the LCMS has largely followed the course set by Johann Walter. Although the days of a single musician having charge of multiple church music programs within a city no longer fit the social context of the New World, the Lutheran musician most likely would have been trained as a schoolteacher, for whom music education and the direction of ecclesiastical liturgical music was an assumed responsibility. In practice, although the United States had favored religious diversity, Lutherans did have a tendency to live in close geographic proximity, creating a social fabric in which a church musician could indeed serve as the larger community's professional musician. These musicians would have had significant training in theology, catechesis, and the classics, as the course lists from the Addison Teachers' Seminary attest.

In Texas, the first usage of the term *Kantor*, with the full implication of its historical meaning, can be traced to Serbin's Carl Teinert, to whom Jan Kilian frequently referred in this official capacity after their arrival in 1854. Indeed, Teinert had been active with Kilian as his musician and a general assistant in Europe as well.[4] Teinert's leadership among the Lutherans both in Saxony and in Texas, as problematic as it sometimes

---

4 The nature of Teinert's partnership with Kilian, particularly in Europe, was certainly nuanced. Kilian referred to Teinert in 1849 as his "chauffeur," but their relationship must have consisted of more substance than

was for Kilian, suggests that in addition to his ability to play organ and violin (likely by ear) and to sing the hymns, Teinert evidenced a fruitful spirituality and a pious Lutheranism. According to Kilian, "He is a Lutheran through and through."[5] His role in establishing new churches with Kilian suggests a sort of nonordained pastoral leadership, and he served for many years on the church council in Serbin, attaining prominence in the small community. He seemed to have no role in teaching music at the Serbin school, but it was at his suggestion for a school nearer to some of the inhabitants of an outlying area that occasioned the congregational split of 1872, eventually resulting in the formation of Holy Cross, Warda, a feat that testifies to Teinert's public status and influence in the community. Considering the historic definition of the office, Teinert was certainly the first Kantor of any Lutheran denomination in Texas, although by nature of his first-generation status, his office must be interpreted generously. There are no records of Teinert composing music for the church or community (while Kilian *did* involve himself in composition). Teinert taught no school music. During these early decades, there is also no mention of a church choir, which one would expect a Kantor in Europe to direct. Yet these considerations could easily have been due to the circumstances in which the early colonists found themselves rather than any willful neglect. Yet Kilian always worked toward implementing a true Kantor position at Serbin.

The congregation's calling of Ernst Leubner as a teacher and Kantor heralded a desire to re-create the professional ecclesiastical office that the Wends had known in Saxony and that represented a move toward the first full-time teacher musician in the Texas LCMS. Unlike Teinert, Leubner was trained in music, the classics, and basic lay church ministry at Addison and

---

this and probably simply reflects Kilian's own autocratic tendencies toward his musician.

5 Kilian, letter to Lindemann, June 26, 1868.

likely would have been prepared to assume his duties in Serbin had the congregation's music corresponded more to his Germanic experience. Nonetheless, neither Teinert nor Leubner would fulfill Kilian's conception of a Lutheran Kantor. Only with the installation of Gerhard Kilian in 1872 would Jan Kilian finally have his Kantor, synodically trained and prepared to teach school, to lead the parish music, and to serve the community as the resident professional musician. Gerhard certainly owed some of his successful lifelong tenure as a beloved musician to Lutherans all throughout Central Texas to Teinert and Leubner, who had paved the way. Whether they were of Wendish extraction or of German background, the value of sacred music was so ingrained in their liturgical piety that these Lutherans expected to sing the great chorales of their faith, led by competent musicians.

Trinity, Houston

Thus, like much of the rest of the LCMS elsewhere, in the first half of the twentieth century, Texas Lutherans established a pattern of the parish's second called worker functioning as a teacher and sacred musician, usually trained at Seward or River Forest. There were, during midcentury, however, stirrings for more from the sacred music vocation. Rev. John William Behnken had served as the pastor at Trinity Lutheran Church in Houston from 1908 until 1935, at which time he ascended to the presidency of the LCMS after a few years as president of the Texas District. As pastor of the church at the time, he certainly must have been involved in the purchase of the Reuter organ in 1921. Following Behnken, Trinity called Rev. Oliver Harms in 1935. Under Harms, who would later also serve as the president of the Texas District and eventually the LCMS, Trinity called Carl Halter in 1937 as "Teacher and Director of Music."[6]

---

6 "Lutherans Stage Conference; Hear Talks by Leaders," *Eagle* (Bryan, TX; April 11, 1942): 3.

This is significant in that Halter had graduated with the equivalent of an associate's degree from River Forest but had stayed an extra year to teach music, and even as an undergraduate, he had demonstrated potential as a musician and a scholar. Trinity had permitted Halter to complete his undergraduate degree during his time there, an opportunity of which he took full advantage, matriculating from Baldwin-Wallace College in Berea, Ohio, in 1941, a student of Albert Riemenschneider. Already a promising scholar, in April 1942, Halter attended a Texas conference of Lutheran pastors and teachers over which national LCMS officials presided and where he offered a lecture dedicated to "Music in the Divine Service," the first recorded instance of a scholarly presentation on sacred music offered by a Lutheran musician in Texas.[7] Later that year, Halter would accept a call to Grace Lutheran, River Forest, and eventually to Concordia, River Forest, where he served in various capacities, from music professor to interim president. His 1963 book *God and Man in Music*, a collection of theological and philosophical essays on church music, likely represents the first instance in the LCMS of a musician publishing theological reflections on church music. During his five-year tenure, Trinity, Houston, had invested in their young schoolteacher and musician, bestowing upon him the title of "Director of Music," a suggestion that his role was more than that of simply organist, and granting him time to pursue his academic studies.

Herbert Garske succeeded Halter at Trinity in 1943. Garske likewise had been born and confirmed in Chicago, graduating from Concordia, River Forest, and the American Conservatory of Music in Chicago, after which time a call to Buffalo, New York, allowed him to study at the Eastman School of Music.[8] Although his service to Trinity was in both teaching and music

---

7　Ibid.

8　"Obituary: Herbert Garske," *Lincoln Journal Star* (April 18, 2009), https://journalstar.com/lifestyles/announcements/obituaries/herbert-e

Figure 7.1 Trinity Lutheran Church in downtown Houston in its previous building. (Source: "Our History," Trinity Lutheran Church Downtown, https://www.trinitydt.org/history/ [accessed February 2, 2022].)

ministries, Garske's musical qualifications were unparalleled in Texas Lutheranism. Rev. Harms must have desired and expected a musician of the highest professional and musical standards, a musician who had achieved beyond the standard training offered to undergraduates. As they had with Halter, Trinity permitted Garske the liberty to pursue his musical interests and the time to engage more in church music when possible. Due to this generous flexibility of employment, no doubt encouraged by Rev. Harms, in 1949, Garske earned a graduate degree in music

-garske/article_cd4a237a-e22a-54cd-9ec1-c02a57188b10.html (accessed October 3, 2020).

Figure 7.2 Carl Halter.
(Source: Courtesy of the
Halter family.)

from Northwestern University.[9] Indeed, it is likely that Garske was the first LCMS musician with a master's degree (in this case, two graduate degrees) to serve full time in Texas. During his over two decades at Trinity, he cofounded the Houston chapter of the American Guild of Organists, oversaw the installation of Trinity's new Holtkamp organ in 1954,[10] performed concerts and organ dedications throughout Texas[11] and directed the music for a convention of the Lutheran Layman's League. In 1953 he coordinated the music for a rally of the International Lutheran Hour, that same year overseeing the music for the LCMS national convention.[12] While still at Trinity, he served as a member of the LCMS Commission on Worship, Liturgics, and Hymnology. In 1964, Garske

9 "N.U. Will Award Honors to 3,581 at Convocation," *Chicago Tribune* (June 12, 1949): 184.

10 "TheHistoryofTrinity'sPipeOrgan,"TrinityDowntown,https://1.cdn.edl .io/hHtZBO6IhLaz2NqO6Qu7oGlU3da0FDftXQRjtk3UZMW7AYff .pdf (accessed October 3, 2020).

11 "Lutherans to Hear Houston Musician," *Fort Worth Star Telegram* (September 2, 1961): 4.

12 "Lutherans Are Preparing for 39th Convention," *Eagle* (Bryan, TX; February 29, 1956): 16.

Figure 7.3 Herbert Garske. (Source: "Obituary: Herbert Garske," *Lincoln Journal Star* [April 18, 2009], https://journalstar.com/lifestyles/announcements/obituaries/herbert-e-garske/article_cd4a237a-e22a-54cd-9ec1-c02a57188b10.html.)

departed Texas for Michigan, where he would teach as a professor of music and humanities at Concordia, Ann Arbor, for twenty years.[13]

Zion, Dallas

In June 1948, Herbert Garske shared organ dedication duties on a two-manual Hammond organ at Trinity Lutheran in Brownsville, Texas.[14] This otherwise inauspicious event on what was surely a disappointing instrument suggests an important connection between Garske, whose professional career as a church musician in the LCMS in Texas had already begun to take shape, and the church's clergyman, Rev. Carl Gaertner, a pastor who offered a unique vision for the Lutheran church musician that was faithful to historic Lutheran practice but also challenged the enduring notion that church musicians were mere contract

---

13 "Obituary: Herbert Garske."
14 "You Are Invited to Hear Herbert Garske, Houston, Texas, in Organ Dedication Concerts," *Brownsville Herald* (Brownsville, TX; June 4, 1948): 2.

workers. Gaertner, born on April 20, 1910, in Port Arthur, Texas, had graduated from St. John's College, Winfield, Kansas, and Concordia Seminary, St. Louis. The Brownsville congregation was Gaertner's second call, following his service from 1934 to 1942 at St. Paul Lutheran Church in Plainview, Texas.[15] Gaertner would have been well acquainted with Trinity in Houston through Rev. Harms, who by 1948 was concluding his role as Texas District vice president and would shortly take up the mantle of Texas District president.[16] Gaertner's long-standing interest in music certainly motivated him to persuade Garske to coperform the dedication concert on Trinity's new Hammond, along with the church's organist, Mrs. N. A. Henderson. Gaertner would have known firsthand of Garske's growing national reputation as a liturgical scholar, church musician, and organ performer—all facets of a professional career that would not have been available to Garske in a less-hospitable environment than Trinity. Gaertner certainly knew that he could never benefit from the services of such a well-qualified church musician in the Kantor tradition, much less someone of national repute, in the far-flung border town of Brownsville, so he would have to wait for the appointed time and place before he could work toward calling such a musician.

In 1951, Rev. Gaertner accepted a call to Zion Lutheran in Dallas. Established in 1879, Zion was the center of North Texas Lutheranism, having birthed the surrounding LCMS churches over the past three-quarters of a century. The church and its school, the first Lutheran parochial school in North Texas, were situated in a leafy and historic neighborhood on Swiss

---

15 Biography from the funeral bulletin, "A Christian Funeral Celebration to the Glory of God and in Memory of the Reverend Carl A. Gaertner," March 20, 1996, Zion Lutheran Church, Dallas.

16 "Oliver Raymond Harms, Seventh President of the Missouri Synod: 1962–1969," Concordia Historical Institute, https://concordiahistorical institute.org/presidents/president-harms/ (accessed October 6, 2020).

Avenue within close proximity to the city center.[17] Gaertner could now utilize the resources of this larger church to implement his vision of a parish music ministry, a vision that fused historic notions of the Lutheran Kantor—intimately integrated into both the church and school, trained to think theologically with a worldview formed by the Lutheran confessions—and the more modern idea of professional specialization, allowing the musician more time to dedicate to church music and to building a program. With this vision in mind, Zion issued a call to Donald Rotermund in 1955 to serve as "Minister of Music and Teacher."[18]

Rotermund was born in St. Louis and graduated from Concordia, River Forest, in 1955 with a teaching degree. From the outset, Gaertner clearly communicated to Rotermund the subtle implications of his unique job title and position. The term *minister of music* might have been an innovation for the LCMS, but it had already found currency in Baptist and Methodist churches in Texas starting around the 1930s and proliferating into the 1940s. Rev. Gaertner would receive criticism from his fellow pastors for such a term for Rotermund's position, terminology they viewed as confusing and problematic—a conflation between ordained and lay ministry. Dr. Paul Westermeyer elucidates the background of this term:

> *Minister of Music* is one term we use in our attempts to point specifically to the church musician's role, but it reflects our confusion. We have often been reminded in our generation that all Christians are *ministers*. Such a definition, though true, leaves us with no notion of why some people are designated as laity and others as clergy. When you consider the

---

17 *The Broadcaster*, church publication of Zion Lutheran Church, Dallas, June 1929. This expanded newsletter, published on Zion's "Golden Jubilee," details the early history of the congregation.

18 Don Rotermund, personal correspondence with the author, October 28, 2020.

distinction, you invariably come to some variation on the theme that ministers in the sense of clergy are responsible for preaching the Word and administering the Sacraments. *Minister of Music* obviously does not fit this definition, so it has to fit a more general sense and suggests that a particular Christian, possibly but not necessarily ordained, is literally responsible for serving up the music.[19]

Westermeyer's exegesis of the term benefits from decades of theologizing and experience since the 1950s; Gaertner's goal was simply to elevate the status of the church musician to encompass a pastoral role, and he understood that words convey meaning. In the 1950s, the title *minister* both evoked and conveyed respect in addition to suggesting pastoral responsibilities, hinting at the old Lutheran term *Kantor*. Westermeyer observes that modern parlance stresses the daily "ministry" of a layperson, all of whom are "ministers." But this shade of meaning doubtlessly has been acquired in the decades hence. The term *Kantor*, which itself bears historical nuance, was not culturally relevant in any meaningful way at the time and was therefore not at Gaertner's disposal. Upon Rotermund's acceptance of the call to Zion, Gaertner communicated clearly that Rotermund's primary duty was as the minister of music rather than as a schoolteacher and that, when circumstances allowed, Rotermund would ideally be relieved of nonmusical teaching in the school in order to devote his energies full time to church and school music.

To Gaertner, Rotermund was "Minister of Music and Teacher" in the same way a church worker could be "Principal and Teacher." The former would receive priority; the latter was secondary, even though for the first years, Rotermund would spend more time teaching school than engaged in church music. Yet Rotermund contends that "Gaertner thought of me

---

19 Westermeyer, *Church Musician*: 16.

first as a musician, then as a teacher," and the respect he was given in subsequent years exemplified this. Following Trinity, Houston's, example of gracious investment in Garske, Rotermund earned his own master's degree in music from what is now the University of North Texas in 1958, Zion permitting him to maintain a flexible schedule to complete his studies. When the church moved to a new location, Rotermund was provided an office with some secretarial help. The move toward a full-time position was achieved only very gradually, and in stages. During the 1970s, Barbara Bradfield, a church member who with her husband, John, had garnered a reputation for promoting quality sacred music at Zion, offered to relieve Rotermund of some of his school responsibilities so that he could devote more time to the thriving music ministry. Bradfield, who offered her services gratis, initially agreed to a two-year commitment, which she subsequently extended for another year. Rotermund credits this, along with secretarial help from church members including Janet Allmon, with allowing him to devote more time to church music. Zion would become a center for church music not only in North Texas but regionally, but that was the result of a community collectively working toward that vision.

In his early years at Zion, Don Rotermund had launched the Dallas Lutheran Acappella Choir, an ensemble inspired by similar notable ventures in Milwaukee and St. Louis, and which, for over a decade, gathered choristers from Lutheran churches across North Texas to sing several programs a year at local churches, allowing these choir members to experience Bach and other composers that were not always practical to perform in their local church choirs. In the late 1950s, Rotermund purchased and assembled a Zuckerman harpsichord for the choir to carry with them when they performed at other churches, whose accompanimental options were sometimes limited. These were the first years of the early music movement, and no doubt this harpsichord was the first such instrument many singers or audiences in the North Texas area had ever experienced. The Dallas Lutheran Acappella Choir would perform a few concerts a year, usually around the church festivals, until Rotermund had to relinquish the choir due to his busy schedule.

Rotermund's attention to church music matters only increased during the 1960s as he supervised the construction of a new organ, designed by Herman Schlicker and installed in Zion's sanctuary in 1969,[20] the first of that firm's instruments in North Texas and for which Paul Manz performed the dedication recital. Even given the cobbled state of the previous organ, Zion had already established itself as a thriving center for concerts, Carl Waldschmidt from Concordia, River Forest, having performed an organ recital at the church in 1957 and Lutheran college choirs routinely performing at Zion on their tours. The church presented Heinrich Fleischer of Rockefeller Memorial Chapel in Chicago in June 1958.[21] The new organ, however, enhanced the quality and scope of programs that could be offered. Zion hosted a "Benderfest" in 1971, featuring music from Jan Bender, then professor of composition at Wittenberg University, but previously of Concordia, Seward, who participated in the proceedings. The church sponsored Paul Manz in a hymn festival in 1972 prior to the Dallas American Guild of Organists convention, during which Marilyn Keiser also performed on the Schlicker organ. Gerhard Schwarz, a German concert organist and professor at the Hochschule für Musik Köln, also played a recital in the 1970s; on another occasion, Richard Wienhorst led a choral workshop. The church even

---

20 Don Rotermund, "A Brief History of the Schlicker/Sipe Organ," single-sheet insert of organ information for a hymn festival in the late 1990s, document in possession of the author.

21 Poster and correspondence related to this concert courtesy of Don Rotermund.

Figure 7.4 Zion's 1969 Schlicker organ in a former sanctuary. (Source: Courtesy of Don Rotermund.)

hosted the Staats- und Domchor from Berlin's cathedral on one of their American tours. By the 1980s, Zion had arguably achieved a reputation as one of the more high-profile churches in the city and was certainly the locus for Lutheran activity, an endeavor aided by its new, modern building with sumptuous acoustics and a generous choir loft. In October 1983, West German president Karl Carstens, in Dallas to promote cultural and business connections between the Federal Republic of Germany and Texas, attended a Sunday-morning divine service at Zion. The choir sang in German a Schütz motet on John 3:16. Rotermund recalled Carstens's thoughtfulness, for "after the service an elder came to the balcony and ushered me to the narthex where he [Carstens] and his wife very warmly expressed their gratitude for the music offered in that service. (It was nice to tell him that the organ case and facade pipes came from Germany.) The preservice security did its search of

Figure 7.5 Paul Manz playing the organ dedication on the Schlicker at Zion, 1969. (Source: Courtesy of Don Rotermund.)

all nooks and closets in the sanctuary, and that included a dog going into the organ case!"[22]

Motivated by the example of the increasingly professional church music programs throughout the state, the Texas District of the LCMS began to notice the vocational parish musician, now an important subset of the pastoral and teaching callings. Lutheran music in Texas, as elsewhere, had been particularly intertwined with that of education. In the 1950s, the Texas District had sponsored an annual, multiday, statewide teachers' conference, the opening service for which often featured choral music. Herbert Garske had directed choirs the first several years of this event, conducted in subsequent years by Don Rotermund. In recognition of the importance of music in the careers of so many Texas District Lutheran schoolteachers, both Garske and Rotermund had been asked to lead sessions

---

22 Don Rotermund, email to the author, October 28, 2020.

for musicians at these early teachers' conferences. Hal Rutz and Bernie Gastler from Austin, as well as others, would teach classes at the conference in subsequent years, all prior to 1965. What had been a rather informal network of Lutheran musicians up until this time would become the Texas District Worship Committee after a district president had inquired whether the group would coordinate worship services for district conventions. At Rotermund's suggestion, clergy were invited to the committee, thus tacitly recognizing the important pastoral work of the church musician—the Kantor, whose task was rooted firmly in a lay ministry of the Word. The committee disseminated a newsletter to congregations in the state, offering historical insights and practical suggestions for the application of music and liturgy. They developed a graded program of devotional liturgies centered on the acronym ACTS (adoration, confession, thanksgiving, supplication) for Lutheran classroom teachers, incorporating elements of prayer, teaching, hymnody, and liturgy. The committee itself sponsored workshops, geared toward pastors' and musicians' mutual interests, around the state.[23] By the time the committee disbanded in the 1990s, it had provided for decades a forum for pastors and musicians to study the history and practice of church music together, certainly inspiring conversations in their home churches.

Recognizing Church Musicians: The Heritage Series

Upon Rev. Gaertner's retirement from Zion, Dallas, in 1976, Rotermund approached Zion's church council with a unique proposal to honor their pastor's ministry through establishing what would become the Heritage Series, an award program that would formally recognize and express appreciation to certain individuals who had served the LCMS in parish music

---

23 Don Rotermund, personal correspondence with the author, October 6, 2020.

Figure 7.6 Zion's Schlicker organ was rebuilt and encased by Robert Sipe for the new sanctuary built in 1982. (Source: "Robert L. Sipe [and Associates] [1982]: Originally Schlicker Organ Co. [1969]," Pipe Organ Database: A Project of the Organ Historical Society, https://pipeorgandatabase.org/organ/36500 [accessed February 2, 2022].)

ministry, akin in some ways to the honorary doctorate in academia. Once a candidate was selected for the Heritage Award, Rotermund would write to the honoree's church council and pastor, informing them of the candidate's selection and offering to pay for the individual's organist substitute for the weekend they would spend in Dallas. Upon arrival in Dallas, the honoree and spouse would attend a small dinner with key church staff on Friday night, while a larger gathering with the congregation happened at Saturday dinner. On Sunday, the individual would often address the Sunday school class, speaking to matters of church music and parish music ministry. The candidate would occasionally play in the Sunday service, or they might possibly compose something for the morning services; indeed, something might have been composed on their behalf for the occasion. Recipients received an organist's stole, a certificate

Figure 7.7 Zion's Heritage Award medallion. (Source: Courtesy of Don Rotermund.)

calligraphed by church member Catherine Burkhard, and a ceramic sculpture in the early days or a "Te Deum" medallion designed by local pastor Harold Jacobsmeyer in later years, all of which would remind the recipient and their congregation both of the honor they had received and of the importance of that individual's music ministry to their home congregation. Rotermund always hoped that the individual's recognition would extend beyond Zion, translating into a greater appreciation from their home parish. Zion presented the first award to Paul Bouman of Grace, River Forest. Subsequent honorees included Gerhardt Becker, longtime musician at St. John's Lutheran in Forest Park, Illinois; Ronald Nelson, a Minnesota-based composer; brothers Harold Albers, Oscar Albers, and George Albers; Herbert and Louis Neuchterlein, for whom both Robert Hobby and Carl Schalk composed pieces for the award; and John Mueller of Holy Cross, Fort Wayne, for whom Mark Bender wrote an anthem. Don Rotermund himself was the recipient in 1995 on the occasion of his fortieth anniversary as minister of music at Zion Lutheran Church and School.

Zion actively commissioned new works through the years, contributing to the *corpus* of sacred music available to subsequent generations. Between 1955 and 1999 alone, the church or individual church members commissioned twenty new works, many of multiple movements, and most published by the Lutheran publishing houses. Commissioned hymn texts include Martin Franzmann's "O Thou Who on th'Accursed Ground" on Rev. Gaertner's twenty-fifth anniversary at Zion and Jaroslav Vajda's "You Are the Rock," prepared for the celebration of Zion's centennial. Paul Manz composed "Two Hymn Improvisations on 'O That I Had a Thousand Voices'" for the dedication of the Schlicker organ in 1969, while Jan Bender composed two sets of organ preludes published by CPH. Choral music comprises the bulk of the commissions. Theodore Beck wrote his "Concertato on 'Jesus, Priceless Treasure'" in gratitude for Zion's minister of education, Wilbert Krause, on his retirement, while Carl Schalk composed a setting of Psalm 25, "Show Me Your Ways," for mixed choir and "Children Are a Gift from God," a musical setting of a text by Zion's principal, Steve Allmon. Walter Pelz composed a concertato on "Oh, That I Had a Thousand Voices," while Richard Hillert wrote his "Prelude/Voluntary/Postlude" for brass, organ, and timpani for the dedication of the new sanctuary in 1982. These commissions frequently honored someone in the congregation, from a professional anniversary as a church worker to a retirement. Several are offered in memory of deceased congregational members or family.[24] Thus was Zion able to solicit the work of some of the great composers of the era while involving congregation members in the project, itself a type of catechesis.

---

24 *Semi-annual Reports: May 23, 1999 Congregational Meeting* (self-pub., 1999).

Figure 7.8 Dr. Don Rotermund. (Source: Courtesy of Don Rotermund.)

The Lutheran Hymn Festival at the Meyerson

With the completion of Dallas's Morton H. Meyerson Symphony Center in 1989 and after the dedication of C. B. Fisk's op. 100, the eighty-four-rank Herman W. and Amelia H. Lay Family Concert Organ in 1992, the Lutheran community of North Texas gathered together to plan a new event that would come to be known simply as the Lutheran Hymn Festival at the Meyerson. Held triennially from 1993, the festival featured a nationally prominent Lutheran organist and a mass SATB choir composed of as many as 150 singers from Lutheran churches, both LCMS and Evangelical Lutheran Church in America, from throughout North Texas. The hymn festival highlighted audience/congregational singing, often featuring *concertato* settings composed by the featured organist himself. Much as Rotermund's Dallas Lutheran Acappella Choir had provided an opportunity for choristers to sing more challenging music than would have been possible in their home parish, the Lutheran Hymn Festival offered an opportunity to sing with fellow Lutherans in the sumptuous acoustics of one of the nation's premiere concert halls, led by one of the finest organs in the state.[25] Although a separate corporate entity from Zion Lutheran Church, the genesis of the Lutheran Hymn Festival was largely due to the lay and pastoral leadership at Zion. Don Rotermund conducted the choirs for the first several hymn festivals. After his retirement, Rotermund's successor as minister of music at Zion, Dr. Sam Eatherton, assumed conducting responsibilities. Dr. Martin Jean served as the first festival organist in 1993, while subsequent organists have included Paul Manz, David Cherwien, Steve Wente, and Jeffrey Blersch.

Where Does Lutheran Sacred Music Stand in Texas Today?

The increasingly interconnected nature of modern American life arguably results in diminished regional differences. Texas is no longer as isolated or as independent as it was in earlier days. Yet Lutheran music in Texas has had to confront certain challenges. Its geographic situation in the midst of the so-called Bible Belt is a mixed blessing. Although Lutheranism in many ways shares a similar worldview with its Baptist or nondenominational neighbors, their unique theological distinctions have resulted in worship expressions congruent with their underlying theology, which is often at odds with historic Lutheranism. Both Prestonwood Baptist in Plano, a megachurch founded in 1977 and currently boasting a membership of 45,000 souls and a weekly attendance of 17,000, and First Baptist Church, Dallas, a historic church which, although only maintaining a third of the membership of the Plano church, has become a center for evangelicalism and conservative politics nationally, have been defining spiritual influences in North Texas. Since 1989, Ed Young's Fellowship Church, based in North Texas with origins

---

25 This author has attended all of them and has written program notes for the last several.

in the Southern Baptist Convention, counts 24,000 in weekly attendance, which includes numerous satellite locations. Joel Osteen's Lakewood Church in Houston, founded in 1999, gathers in what was once a sports arena, from which he presides over a media empire that, through books and television, reaches millions of people per week. These influential establishments have generated their fair share of nondenominational franchise congregations whose theology and worship style imitate the success of their larger brethren, in either case drinking from the well of Charles Finney's New Measures, enticing a spiritual experience out of even the most unwitting observer through an admixture of winsome, self-help-styled preaching, theatrical effects, and the highest level of commercial musical production.

These churches cannot but have an effect on the Lutheran community in Texas, but one must cautiously assert that not all their influence has been negative in the realms of music and worship. These franchise megachurches have championed professionalism and spared no expense in hiring the right staff for their productions, which cannot be rivaled by the average neighborhood parish. From this writer's experience in the northern suburbs of Dallas, the LCMS congregations struggled throughout the 1990s and into the 2000s in their philosophical approach to worship. In fact, the presence of these megachurches *forced* pastors and musicians, particularly in suburban communities, to confront their Lutheran identity. In many cases, congregants forced the matter on church staff who had to acquiesce or engage in a serious program of catechesis, themselves having to usurp the role of apologists for Lutheran liturgical identity. Some congregations answered these challenges by establishing "blended" worship featuring choir and organ and praise band all within the same service. Some have elected to offer both "contemporary" and "traditional" services, dividing the congregation by worship preference. As time has sorted out these questions, a few Texas LCMS churches have abandoned any semblance of Lutheran worship traditions, occasionally even jettisoning any public mention of their denominational affiliation. But many other congregations have intentionally decided to offer something the surrounding ecclesiastical culture cannot give by offering authentic Lutheran worship in Word and Sacrament. This process was hastened by the rapid adoption of the *Lutheran Service Book* in 2006, which, unencumbered by sanctimonious nostalgia and handicapping antipathy, offered a neutral choice for all but the most rabid partisans on either side of the spectrum. In only a few years, this writer's congregation at the time went from simultaneously using *The Lutheran Hymnal*, *The Other Song Book*, and a smattering of choruses to adopting the *Lutheran Service Book* and its liturgies, complete with chanting and singing the psalms.[26]

The position of the professional Kantor, in whatever terminology a congregation elects to employ, and here suggesting a professional without nonmusic teaching responsibilities in the parochial school, is a relatively new vocation for the LCMS. Michael Zehnder recalls,

> In 1984, I was on the LCMS DCE roster. I had received a call from St John's Lutheran Church in Orange, California, to be their first full-time minister of music. (Dave Held, who went to Seward to become a music professor previously, held the music position but he also had other non-musical duties and had to do much of the school music.) I called Dale Griffin at the LCMS office and asked how many positions of this type even existed in the Synod. He told me he was going to ask around and then call me back, stating that at the time they didn't keep such records. When he did call back he informed me that in talking to other church leaders in the LCMS office

---

26 Lord of Life Lutheran Church, LCMS, in Plano, Texas, 1993–2017, Rev. John Lindner being pastor here for most of the time.

they could only identify ten or eleven such full-time music positions that even existed in our Synod.[27]

As groundbreaking as Don Rotermund's minister of music position at Zion, Dallas, was intended to be in the late 1950s, Rotermund himself nevertheless maintained some nonmusical teaching responsibilities at the school until a few years before his retirement in 1999, only by the end of his career undoubtedly fulfilling Gaertner's vision of a minister of music by devoting himself to the church's music full time. The church musician's vocation was steadily moving away from its historic ties with the parochial schoolteacher.

The career of Richard Leslie, another longtime Lutheran church musician in Texas, tells the story of another path toward full-time sacred music in Texas. Leslie, who graduated in 1970 from Missouri State University, majoring in organ performance and choral conducting, served LCMS churches in Michigan and Illinois before accepting a call in as director of Christian education in 1986 to Gloria Dei Lutheran Church in the Houston suburb of Nassau Bay, where his job originally involved overseeing adult education and all facets of a growing music ministry. Gloria Dei had been led at the time by Rev. John Kieschnick, a prominent Lutheran cleric who represented a different strand of Lutheranism in Texas. Kieschnick, himself a descendent of the Wends, shepherded a congregation in the shadow of the Johnson Space Center, counting prominent scientists and astronauts on its membership rolls. At one point, the church claimed around 3,300 members, a success claimed in spite of their Lutheran identity rather than because of it. Kieschnick observed in 2009 that "we are Lutheran, but we don't make a big deal out of that. It is not that we are embarrassed, but that to us is not the important thing. The main thing

---

27 Michael Zehnder, personal correspondence with the author, September 22, 2020.

is to bring people to know Jesus Christ."[28] The Church Growth Movement of the 1980s had influenced Kieschnick, who, according to Leslie, believed that growing churches should employ less liturgical and traditional forms of ritual. Yet this same movement had also encouraged senior pastors to value their musicians—indeed, all of their staff—in a professional and ministerial sense, in much the same way as Rev. Gaertner had envisioned for his called musician at Zion, Dallas, in 1955. Thus, early in his tenure at Gloria Dei, Leslie had not only completed colloquy in the LCMS; he had been relieved of DCE responsibilities in order to become its first "Minister of Music and Celebration," allowing him to focus solely on parish music. Leslie remembered that "John Kieschnick insisted that his staff were part of his ministry. The spiritual authority of those working on staff was an outgrowth of his authority as senior pastor. In this way, he was convinced the church would grow. However, this meant he put his staff to work! The Minister of Music [and Celebration] would be the first ministerial contact for music people. These were joyous times!"[29] More traditional Lutherans may decry aspects of the Church Growth Movement, but its emphasis on the value of a professional staff to the modern church arguably acclimated many more traditional LCMS churches to the benefits and respectability of a full-time parish musician. Kieschnick thought liturgical worship to be of limited value to the modern church and charged Leslie to research and write a "theological prospectus" based specifically on extrapolating the fundamental principles enshrined in Luther's *Deutsche Messe* (1526) and the *Formulae Missae* (1523), the results of which would guide worship practices at

28 Richard Vara, "Gloria Dei Lutheran Church Is under a New Shepherd; to Add Second Campus," *Houston Chronicle* (November 10, 2007), https://www.chron.com/life/houston-belief/article/Gloria-Dei-Lutheran-Church-is-under-a-new-1828144.php (accessed November 8, 2021).

29 Richard Leslie, personal correspondence with the author, October 18, 2021.

Gloria Dei. As a result, the congregation was at the forefront in strategically offering services utilizing different amounts of traditional liturgy to attract different worshipping audiences, resulting in an early service of "high liturgy" (faithfully from the hymnal), a middle service introducing less traditional elements, with the late service fully "contemporary." Although this arrangement of Sunday service styles is somewhat conventional now, Gloria Dei's practices served as an example to many Lutheran churches in Texas and beyond. While the theological merits of Gloria Dei's worship practices have been debated within the context of the "worship wars" of subsequent decades, the fact that Leslie was entrusted with this task by the senior pastor demonstrates not only mutual respect between pastor and musician but the value the senior pastor placed on music in congregational life. Although Rev. Gaertner of Zion, Dallas, and Rev. Kieschnick of Gloria Dei, Houston, nurtured very different liturgical and musical visions for their congregations, both resulted in the creation of full-time parish musician positions, each in its own way elevating and normalizing the status of professional musicians. Although representing dissimilar liturgical expressions, both congregations manifested an early trajectory toward full-time parish music positions in the LCMS during the last quarter of the twentieth century, valuing as they did their liturgical musicians who would play an integral role in the ministry of the Word.

In 2020, of the approximately 360 congregations in the LCMS in Texas, about 26 employ some type of musician full time. In several cases, they are also responsible for parochial school music, but in no case does their job description include teaching nonmusical subjects. This does include a few instances of ordained clergy who are also responsible for the parish music, these instances attesting to the creativity of churches—and individuals—who have innovatively sought solutions to allow full-time attention to parish music.

Here must be made an uncomfortable distinction simply for matters of accounting—this discussion centers on full-time musicians. Of course, this is not to dismiss the part-time musicians who continue to serve at almost every congregation of the LCMS in Texas. These musicians, sometimes volunteer and sometimes paid a mere pittance, are still the stalwarts of church music, much as Carl Teinert found time to make music on the organ and violin in between farming and raising children. Yet it is easier to track the growth of churches and the liturgical visions of congregations when considering how many have elected to expand their investment into their music programs that a full-time person certainly does represent.

Perhaps these distinctions offer other insights. Not all of these twenty-six individuals are necessarily synodically trained or rostered, but neither was Ivan Olson when Concordia College hired him to teach in 1952. These modern-day musicians may serve primarily as guitarists or song leaders, coordinating the music in "contemporary" congregations, or they may be trained as traditional "organist/choirmaster" types, playing the organ and directing a graded choral program. The skills required for each of these jobs are not necessarily interchangeable. Although there are always exceptions, most organists/choirmasters cannot read chord charts or play guitar, even if they do enjoy other styles of music. Similarly, playing the great hymns of the church on the organ at a service adorned with the chorale preludes of Bach, for example, are not necessarily skills the praise band musician has sought to develop. In the days of the teacher/musician, most had trained at a Concordia and were taught to play the hymns and the liturgy, if not in the same way, then at least with a uniform understanding as to what hymns and liturgy they would have to play. Kilian's *Choralbuch* was necessary precisely because his people sang hymns differently than the LCMS sang them or taught them at Addison. The adoption of the *Lutheran Service Book* aside, the LCMS is certainly less uniform in its liturgical practice now than it was earlier in the twentieth century, and that progression will certainly continue to inform the development of parish musicians. If the LCMS is losing members, it is not true that every church is shrinking. Many of the larger ones are growing. Churches that could once afford a full-time musician can sometimes now barely afford part-time musicians, while larger churches are, in fact, employing multiple musicians to handle different "styles" of worship even on different campuses. Will this only exacerbate a potential rift between musicians employed full time and those only part time, but otherwise equally qualified? There exists plenty of challenge in the coming years.

The lessons from those Texas Lutheran musicians of long-gone days can perhaps guide us on the path yet to be trod. The early Lutheran immigrants had few musical resources, but they paid heed to their church music as soon as it was possible. They placed music *next* to the Word of God in its importance to their divine services, but there was never any doubt that they would sing hymns from the hymnal led by an instrument of some kind, even if they had to inhabit the state for almost forty years before an LCMS church could claim an actual pipe organ. The Anglican spoken service represented a foreign tradition, and even the most rustic Lutheran worship service would include hymns. Although music may look different in various places, one would be hard-pressed to find a Lutheran congregation that intentionally omitted music from its services. If there is any salve to the wounds earned in various of the worship wars of recent years, it is that many of these early Texas Lutherans experienced similar strife. Wendish or German? German or English? To sing the hymns isometrically or rhythmically? These cultural antagonisms are not merely characteristics of the nineteenth century. Even as late as 1958 at Holy Cross, Warda, "singing was done in both languages [English and German], with English becoming more popular

over the years. For a while, hymns were even sung in both languages at the same time by members of the congregation."[30] If
this holy cacophony bore the imprint of Pentecost, it still represents the deep-seated need for people to express their prayer,
praise, and proclamation in a familiar piety. The fervency with
which one holds their sacred music traditions then as now is
often intensely personal—although, one would also have to
note that these conflicts in the past were largely centered on
how to sing, not *what* to sing. With some variety allowed for
different geographic traditions, Texas Lutherans always sang
from the Lutheran chorale tradition and thus could be assured
that Lutheran doctrine would be promulgated from one generation to the next. Does the diversity of worship practices these
days call into question whether this is still the case?

These Texas Lutherans, like those elsewhere, valued
advanced training in their musicians, echoing Luther: "Necessity demands that music be kept in schools. A schoolmaster
must know how to sing; otherwise I do not look at him. And
before a youth is ordained into the ministry, he should practice music in school."[31] Those early Texas Lutherans knew they
could not train or mentor church musicians in situ, generally
relying on the Addison Seminary, or later one of the other Concordias, to provide professional training until they could found
their own college in Austin. Pedagogy and church music were
seen as inexorably conjoined, a professional notion that developed through the twentieth century, whereby, for better or for
worse, the schoolteacher now seldom serves as the Kantor and
vice versa. One can lament that Lutheran schoolteachers are no
longer taught organ specifically and church music in general,
but one can also likewise rejoice that there are now professional

---

30 *125 Years of God's Grace*: 37.
31 Ewald M. Plass, trans., *What Luther Says: An Anthology* (St. Louis, MO:
CPH, 1994): 980. See also Martin Luther, *Luthers Werke: Tischreden*, 6
Vols. (Weimar: H. Böhlau, 1912–21): 5:557.

Kantors who have been specially trained and can devote their full-time energies to shepherding the congregation's music ministries.

The witness of these Texas Lutherans demonstrates a community that believed in the primal importance of music in church life. That there has been controversy as to its proper liturgical application simply amplifies the truth in Martin Luther's observation that "next to the Word of God, music deserves the highest praise. She is a mistress and governess of those human emotions. . . . No greater commendation than this can be found—at least not by us. For whether you wish to comfort the sad, to terrify the happy, to encourage the despairing, to humble the proud, to calm the passionate, or to appease those full of hate . . . what more effective means than music could you find?"[32] The personal and community energy these early Lutherans expended to ensure that people could sing the Word of God through hymns, led by properly trained musicians, should encourage later generations as they continue that consequential task of producing sacred music. During a time in which the sad, the jovial, the despairing, the conceited, the raving, and even perhaps the "hate-filled" need the grace offered by the gospel, proper sacred music can now, as then, offer solace and consolation to all who would receive.

---

32 Martin Luther, *Luther's Works*, American ed., Vols. 1–30, ed. Jaroslav Pelikan (St. Louis, MO: Concordia, 1955–76); Vols. 31–55, ed. Helmut Lehmann (Philadelphia: Fortress, 1957–86): 53:323.

Epilogue

Lutheran sacred musicians in Texas in the early years exemplified the heights of perseverance, their challenges nuanced by the times in which they lived, but certainly offering principles to apply today. Perhaps James 5:11 is relevant to this narrative: "Behold, we consider those blessed who remained steadfast. You have heard of the steadfastness of Job, and you have seen the purpose of the Lord, how the Lord is compassionate and merciful." Even at its best, Texas offered an inhospitable environment for the early settlers, requiring the utmost tenacity. From droughts and floods, to snakes and other wild perils, to recalcitrant native populations, and to the challenge of utilizing the many natural resources of the land before the development of modern technologies, these early Lutherans might have been forgiven had they resolved to establish a viable means of livelihood in the post oaks and prairies before they turned their attentions to their spiritual lives. Yet the practice of their Christian faith had been so integrated into their lives that the Lutheran colonies in Texas collectively built churches as their first public buildings. Further, there was never any question that worshippers would express their faith through hymns within the liturgy. Perhaps this represents a decidedly pre-twentieth-century mindset, in which the cultural and spiritual values of Christianity are now challenged by a secular culture. These Lutherans considered congregational singing fundamental to their liturgies; this singing represented not mere entertainment but rather the "work of the people." In fact, choirs are seldom mentioned in the earliest Texas congregations, as the people, of course, functioned as the choir. Even instruments meant to lead the congregation in their singing—usually an organ, piano, or violin—were simply auxiliary to and meant to enhance the congregation's voice. At what point do the luxuries and accoutrements of the modern music ministry distract from the worthy goal of congregational singing?

Indeed, these early Lutherans embraced a vision of a liturgical praxis in which congregational song predominated. Some may have known a more sophisticated liturgical and musical life in Europe, but their vision was not clouded by the impractical when they arrived in the New World. Kilian's earliest job description for his cantor included the ability to lead singing, not only with the organ, but with his voice. He needed to be able to sing the hymns in the way that people knew them, all to the end that the congregation might be freed to sing. As glorious as the Lutheran choral tradition had been in Europe, the early settlers were not compelled to establish choirs to execute weekly cantatas in accordance with the church year. Their lean existence in Texas meant forgoing such niceties in favor of congregational singing, which, after all, had been a central component of the choral cantatas anyway. In the New World, these Lutherans were still propelled by a liturgical vision that gave hymn singing primary importance. In Europe, congregational singing had been adorned by complex choral and instrumental settings; in Texas, with the adornments stripped away, hymn singing was still as important to the liturgy. Maintaining this vision required flexibility—not a trait that Lutherans are generally known to possess in great abundance. To keep the practice of their Lutheranism at the forefront of their lives required the ability to adapt to the challenging circumstances of life in Texas.

Alluding to James 5:11 again, one can easily discern the blessings from God that resulted from their faithfulness. Growth in numbers of congregations, in the number of souls, and increasing connections with Lutherans throughout the United States certainly could be interpreted as God's blessing. But with success comes distractions. One could argue that much of Christianity in the mid-twentieth century both benefited from and was hindered by its prevalent cultural acceptance. Churches awash with money and overflowing with attendance, choirs and music ministries burgeoning with children, youth, and adults alike—these may have been abundant times, but how much of the success represents the legacy of "cultural" Christianity? The sacrifice and faithfulness of the early immigrants had resulted in great successes for Texas Lutheranism, whereby even synod presidents would routinely hail from the state. And in matters of sacred music and the training of church musicians, Texas Lutherans continued to adapt while striving to keep the gospel foremost.

Church musicians in modern times have likewise had to exhibit great flexibility and fortitude. Differing ideas of what constitutes sacred music have required musicians to become diplomats and theologians as they offer pastoral care to their parishioners. Musicians must be able to articulate their own vision for music ministry to congregants who may have their own embedded ideas of what constitutes good church music, whether or not they are theologically systematized. Just as Kilian had to mediate between the factions and warring national identities in his own parish, how often does the modern pastor or musician have to navigate their own precipitous way amid various currents of opinions? It should be a comfort to know that previous generations have engaged in these same struggles.

Just as these early Lutherans had to exhibit adaptability while pursuing a spiritual vision in the New World, the modern church has had to adjust to the sweeping changes brought about by a pandemic. From the reduction of choirs and singing to transitioning to online platforms, church musicians had to think in new ways that their forebears never would have been able to contemplate but that exemplify the same flexibility. How does one offer Word and Sacrament with only limited opportunities to meet in person? This situation required of churches that they consider whether sacred music can be disposed of or whether, in the words of Luther, music is "next to theology" in importance. In what ways could music still serve as the handmaid to theology when services were largely online, and congregants' sole means of participation in the liturgy was often through their computer screens? Through utmost ingenuity, many pastors and musicians found solutions that were able to provide the consolation of the gospel coupled with offering the comfort of familiar sung hymns and liturgy. As with those Lutherans of old who refused to be bound by the tyranny of perfection, adapting their sacred music to the resources at hand, so too were so many modern musicians able to transition to media, which, while neither ideal nor proper for a long-term expression of the divine service, still clearly communicated the gospel, albeit through the impersonal computer screen. This could never replace Christians meeting together, but the flexibility these clergy and musicians demonstrated in utilizing these imperfect vehicles to accomplish the important task of nourishing people with the gospel certainly hearkens back to the creativity of those early Texan Lutheran settlers.

Thus is the story of Lutheran music in Texas one of forbearance, adaptability, and commitment to a vision of Word and Sacrament that upholds sacred music as a vehicle for the proclamation of the gospel; it is the story of generations who practiced and advocated for a corporate spirituality, borne from the Lutheran confessions, in which the church was central to their communities. Theirs is not a story of perfection, however; their disagreements were legion. From congregational factions, to ethnic prejudices, to intensely personal battles over musical styles, to an insular parochialism that sometimes hindered the free preaching of the gospel, to struggling with compromises in education, these early Texan Lutherans engaged in those common human struggles that result from sin. In many ways, their failures and successes are no more unique than those of Lutherans throughout the world. Yet Texas, with its fiercely independent spirit, rugged individualism, and general detachment from the technology and civilization characteristic of elsewhere in the United States, resulted in the development of a Lutheranism distinct to the state. Through the disappointments, achievements, and anointed experiences of these prior generations, however, the Lord's "compassion and mercy" has been evident throughout, utilizing sacred music, and those who were skilled to sing and to play, to build and uphold his kingdom in the Lone Star State.